PLAIN ENGLISH FOR DRAFTING STATUTES AND RULES

PLAIN ENGLISH FOR DRAFTING STATUTES AND RULES

ROBERT J. MARTINEAU
DISTINGUISHED RESEARCH PROFESSOR OF LAW, EMERITUS
UNIVERSITY OF CINCINNATI

ROBERT J. MARTINEAU, JR.
COMMISSIONER
TENNESSEE DEPARTMENT OF ENVIRONMENT AND CONSERVATION

ISBN: 978-1-4224-9914-6

Library of Congress Cataloging-in-Publication Data

Martineau, Robert J.
Plain English for drafting statutes and rules / Robert J. Martineau, Robert J. Martineau, Jr.
p. cm.
Includes index.
ISBN 978-1-4224-9914-6
1. Legal composition--United States. 2. Bill drafting--United States 3. Legislation--United States. 4. Administrative regulation drafting--United States. 5. Law--United States--Interpretation and construction. 6. Statutes--United States. I. Martineau, Robert J., Jr. II. Title.
KF250.M365 2012
352.80973--dc23   2012030562

NOTE TO USERS
To ensure that you are using the latest materials available in this area, please be sure to periodically check the LexisNexis Law School web site for downloadable updates and supplements at www.lexisnexis.com/lawschool.

Editorial Offices
121 Chanlon Rd., New Providence, NJ 07974 (908) 464-6800
201 Mission St., San Francisco, CA 94105-1831 (415) 908-3200
www.lexisnexis.com

MATTHEW◆BENDER

FOREWORD

For the third time Professor Martineau, now joined by his son Robert J. Martineau, Jr., as co-author, has prepared a guide for drafting a statute or rule in Plain English. This book arises out of the experiences of both authors in the teaching of legislative drafting skills to both law students and professional drafters and extensive experience in drafting constitutional provisions, statutes, and administrative and court rules at all levels of government — federal, state, and local. It is based on the principles of Plain English as well as rules that govern the preparation of statues and rules.

While the basic approach of Plain English continues in this book, it incorporates substantial differences from the previous books as well as other advocates of Plain English. First, it expressly builds on the work of Jeremy Bentham, who first developed the core principles of drafting statutes in Plain English at the end of the 18th century, as well as that of E. B. White and William Zissner in 20th Century, who stressed the importance of the simple declarative sentence as a key component of clear writing.

We address this book to two audiences. The first is law students who are introduced to legal writing in their first year but usually are never called upon to engage in the discipline of structured writing that statute and rule drafting requires. The second is the lawyer (or even non-lawyer) who drafts a statute or rule as a staff member of a legislative committee, legislative drafting service, government agency, private organization, bar association, or private client.

In the modern world, statutes and rules play an ever-increasing role in the lives of almost every person. For this reason it now more important than ever for those who draft these statutes and rules to be able to make them as readable and understandable as possible. That is the goal of this book.

This book could not, of course, been written without the assistance of a number of people. At the University of Cincinnati College of Law, Dean Louis Bilionis was most supportive both financially and in offering encouragement. Assistant Dean James Schoenfeld was generous in ironing out practical details, and recent graduate Sarah Dwider, who assisted in the early research.

A special note of thanks is due to our research assistant, University of Cincinnati law student Krista Johnson. Not only did she do the usual type of research, she did much more — editing, finding examples of poorly drafted statutes and rules for the drafting exercises. She was also invaluable in converting all of the written material into the documents that were sent to our publisher. All of this did promptly and efficiently, while continuing as both a law student and law review staff member.

Robert J. Martineau
Robert J. Martineau, Jr.

(Disclaimer note: The view express in this book are those of the authors only and do not necessarily reflect those of the State of Tennessee or its Department of Environment and Conservation.)

DEDICATION

To our families, especially our wives Connie and Pam, without whose love and support this book could not have been written

TABLE OF CONTENTS

Table of Contents

Table of Contents

Table of Contents

Table of Contents

Table of Contents

PART I

WHY STATUTORY AND RULE DRAFTING IS SO POOR AND HOW TO IMPROVE IT

Lawyers have two common failings. One is that they do not write well. The other is that they think they do.[1]

---

[1] Felsenfeld, *The Plain English Movement in the United States*, 6 Canadian Business Law Journal 413 (1981-82).

Chapter 1

THE NEVER ENDING STRUGGLE

A. THE HISTORIC PROBLEM OF POOR LEGAL DRAFTING

The problem of poor legal drafting goes back as far as there has been a legal profession. The reasons for it start with historic — the use of Latin and then a combination of Latin and French in legal documents following the Norman conquest of England in 1066. More simply, critics just blame lawyers. As one stated, "[l]awyers have two common failings. One is that they do not write well, and the other is that they think they do."[2] In saying this, he was echoing the comment made by Reed Dickerson, one of the first critics of the legal writing skills of both lawyers and law professors, that each group not only considers its members well-trained and expert legal drafters, but do not see writing inadequacies in other lawyers or law professors.[3]

We agree with both critics. We make this acknowledgely harsh judgment on the basis of a combined 75 years experience drafting constitutional, statutory, and rule provisions, writing appellate briefs, teaching writing skills to law students and legal professionals, as well as writing many books and law review articles. We also believe that part of the fault lies in our educational system, both pre-legal and legal.

In elementary (not coincidentally once known as grammar schools) and high schools, the role of English grammar, composition, and now even cursive writing have given way to all students being given the notebook version of a computer, eliminating the need for books and pencil and paper. These developments are not new. It was over a half century ago that Rudolph Flesch published his famous critique of primary education *Why Johnny Can't Read*. Since then, we have gone through the 1970s with open, unstructured classrooms with the focus on creative writing to the current teaching to the standardized test mandated by the "No Child Left Behind" Act that involves only a check in a box for an answer. Things are no better at the college level, where many if not most students can graduate without ever having written a paper or been faced with an exam that requires an essay answer.

The situation in law schools has traditionally been even worse. The mandatory first year legal research and writing course gives the illusion of teaching good legal writing skills without really doing so. The reasons for this failure are several-fold. First is the structure of the courses. Most of them call for a two credit course in each semester. The first semester includes legal research — how to use the law library and do legal research online. Attention is then given to legal writing, often with emphasis on the

---

[2] *Id.*

[3] R. Dickerson, Legislative Drafting 3-4 (1954).

KISS (Keep It Simple, Stupid) principle. Students then write a short legal memorandum. The second semester is devoted to a moot court program in which the student writes a brief and makes a short oral argument in an appeal from a trial court decision, the "record" being only a two or three page summary of the lower court proceedings. Needless to say, the total amount of attention given to the legal writing aspect of the course is so limited as to be next to useless.

A further problem is the quality of the instructors in these courses. In many if not most law schools, they are recent law school graduates who have not yet practiced and who hold the position for only a year or two. Few have any experience in teaching writing skills or anything else. There is a minority of law schools that do have instructors who make a career of the position, but often they do not have full faculty status.[4] The result is, as might be expected, that most law students learn little about good legal writing in the first year. The fault is not in the instructors. They do the best they can. The fault lies in the system and especially in those in charge of the system. This is not surprising in light of Dickerson's comment noted above that most law professors consider themselves excellent legal writers.

There are additional opportunities in the second and third years, such as courses in legal writing (especially those using Richard Wydich's *Plain English for Lawyers*), courses in legislative drafting, as well as law review, but these reach only a small minority of law students. For the large majority, eight or ten hours of classroom instruction in legal writing by a neophyte instructor is all they are going to get. This situation fully justifies the criticism quoted above that the problem is that lawyers do not write well but think they do. Even worse, it supports Dickerson's further criticism that since law school professors do not see a problem with the legal writing skills of themselves or other lawyers, they see no reason for the law schools to do anything to correct the problem other than to let those few professors (and practitioners) who think there is a problem propose and teach a course in legal or legislative drafting.

One effort to improve the teaching of legal writing and the status of those who do it is the Legal Writing Institute, founded in 1984. It has publishesd The Journal of the Legal Writing Institute since 1988. An older organization, The American Society of Legal Writers, has a somewhat broader focus, legal writing in general. It publishes The Scribes Journal of Legal Writing.

B. EFFORTS TO IMPROVE LEGAL DRAFTING

In a curious twist, the effort to improve the quality of legal drafting in general began in the United States with the effort to improve legislative and rule drafting. Rudolph Flesh's first book in 1946, *The Art of Plain Talk*, was an an attack on the poor drafting of federal administrative rules affecting consumers. This defect made the rules difficult for consumers, the intended beneficiaries of the rules, to know and enforce their rights under the rules. To the same effect was his 1979 book *How to Write Plain English: A Book for Lawyers and Consumers*. Reed Dickerson's first book,

---

[4] There are exceptions, including the University of Cincinnati. For a review of efforts to give legal writing instructors faculty status, see Weresh, *Form and Substance: Standards for Promotion and Retention of Legal Writing Faculty on Clinical Tenure Track*, 37 Golden Gate U. L. Rev. 281 (2007).

published in 1954, was *Legislative Drafting*. It was not until 1965 that he published *Fundamentals of Legal Drafting*, which was a project of the American Bar Foundation.

Since these early efforts, there has been a host of books and articles on improving legal drafting. While several of them focus on legislative and rule drafting, most of them have legal drafting in general or some aspect of drafting private legal documents such as contracts as their main focus. The best known is Wydick's *Plain English for Lawyers*. The largest publisher of books for lawyers lists over 20 books on legal drafting in its catalog, only one of which is on legislative and rule drafting.

Some federal agencies have gotten into the act. The Securities and Exchange Commission, for example, adopted rules in 1998 and 2006 requiring the use of Plain English in prospectuses and certain types of disclosure filings with the SEC. Individual states have adopted similar requirements for insurance policies and other types of consumer documents.

How successful have these efforts been? One indicator may be the form contract for the sale of real estate issued in 2010 jointly by the Florida State Bar (a body under the supervision of the Florida Supreme Court) and the Florida Board of Realtors. The contract is 11 pages long, contains 600 lines, and averages over 15 words per line, for a total word count of almost 10,000 words. A contract of this length, intended to be signed by persons with little or no experience in real estate, has a host of legal implications that are far beyond the understanding of those who sign it, not to mention the real estate agents presenting it for signature. At the very least, the contract requires each party to have its own attorney, something not usual in most real estate transactions that involve only private residences. (Of course, changing that situation may be the goal of the contract, at least from the perspective of the Florida Bar.)

C.   THE SPECIAL PROBLEMS OF STATUTORY AND RULE DRAFTING

As bad as the state of legal writing in general is, the sorry state of statutory and rule drafting is far worse. The problem has, of course, the same root cause as poor legal drafting in general — the almost universal misconception of lawyers that they are expert legal drafters, as explained in the two previous sections. When it comes to statutory and rule drafting, however, the evils that flow from a poorly drafted statute or rule in most instances dwarf those that flow from a poorly drafted private legal document such as a contract. This is because a private legal document usually affects only a limited number of people, most of whom voluntarily become parties to the contract. They have an opportunity before being bound by the contract to review its terms and make a choice whether to enter the contract and to have legal advice when doing so. With a statue or rule, however, only a few of those affected by it have participated in its preparation, but all must comply with its provisions. Under these circumstances, the ability of these people — the public — to understand their rights and duties under the statute or rule is fundamental to its effectiveness. It is not too much of an overstatement to say that due process in the sense of notice requires that a statute or rule be written clearly enough so that those affected by it can read it and understand their rights and duties under it.

The notion that a statute or rule must be written in language that the general public can understand has ancient origins. One of the first, the Statute of Pleadings, was enacted in 1362. Even though the statute itself was written in French, it required that pleas filed in court be "pleaded, shewed, defended, answered, debated, and judged in the English Tongue." It was not until 1489, however, that all English statutes were written in English. Even that preceded the adoption of English as the language of legal documents in 1649.[5]

In light of this history in England, it is not surprising that at the time of the American Revolution, important players such as John Adams and Thomas Jefferson criticized the language used in statutes. Adams called for "common sense in common language" in statutes, clearly a precursor of the Plain English movement. Jefferson was particularly forceful when he described statutes

> *which from their verbosity, their endless tautologies, their involutions of case within case, and parenthesis within parenthesis, and their multiplied efforts at certainty by saids and aforesaids, by ors and by ands, to make them more plain, do really render them more perplexed and incomprehensible, not only to common readers, but to lawyers themselves.*[6]

The first effort to improve the quality of the drafting of statutes began in England by Jeremy Bentham at the end of the 18th century. In one of his many writings, *View of a Complete Code of Laws*, first published in 1843, some 11 years after his death but written much earlier, he called not only for the substitution of a code of laws for the common law, but gave detailed instructions of how the code should be drafted. Key to the whole enterprise was that the code be drafted in language the common person could understand. As he put it, laws should not be in *"any other legal terms than such as are familiar to the people."* If it is necessary to use technical terms, they should be defined in the law in *"common and known words."*[7] He also gave detailed instructions as to drafting style. These are discussed below in Chapters 10 and 12. As will be seen, his views on drafting style are very similar to the principles of Plain English as they have developed in the past half century. It is not an exaggeration to identify Bentham as the father, or perhaps the grandfather, of the Plain English movement.

Unfortunately, Bentham had little effect on the manner in which English statutes were drafted. The next effort was by George Coode in his book *Legislative Expression: or, the Language of the written Law*, published in 1845. He developed the notion of a statute involving a legal subject and a legal action, again a precursor of the Plain English movement's the "Who" and the "What." His other major contribution was to condemn the use of the proviso, advocating the placement of conditions at the beginning of the sentence rather than adding a proviso at the end of the sentence, a staple of Plain English style. Following him was Thring's *Practical Legislation*,

---

[5] Ormond, *The Use of English: Language, Law, and Political Culture in Fourteenth-Century England*, 78 Speculum 750 (2003).The most extensive treatment of the transition from French to English in English legal proceedings and statutes is D. Mellinkoff, The Language of the Law 95-135 (2004).

[6] Mellinkoff, *supra* note 5, at 253.

[7] J. Bentham, Works 209 (Bowring, ed., 1843).

published in 1877, and Ilbert's *Legislative Methods and Form*, published in 1901. The next major work, this time in Canada, was Driedger's *Composition of Legislation*, first published in 1957.

As noted above, the first efforts in the United States to improve statute and rule drafting were Dickerson's *Legislative Drafting*, published in 1954, and Flesch's 1956 book *The Art of Plain Talk*. Notwithstanding this early focus, until recently, most attention in the United States has been on improving legal drafting generally, with no special focus on statute and rule drafting. All but a few of the books published on the drafting skills of lawyers in the past thirty years, including those advocating the use of Plain English, have ignored statute and rule drafting as a special form of legal drafting. The first major effort to combine Plain English with statute and rule drafting was the Law Reform Commission of Victoria, Australia, which published a report, Plain English and the Law, in 1987. The authors' book *Drafting Legislation and Rules in Plain English* published in 1991 was, in fact, the first comprehensive treatment of the subject in book form in the United States.

While there have been limited efforts to improve the drafting of legislation, there has been an effort to require that the rules adopted by federal administrative agencies be written in common or plain language. The first one often cited is an order supposedly issued by President Nixon in 1972 that required the Federal Register be written in "layman's terms," but this claim is of dubious validity.[8] The first formal executive order on the subject was No. 12044 issued by President Carter in 1978 mandating that federal regulations be "as simple and clear as possible . . . written in plain English . . . and understandable to those who must comply with it." President Carter in 1979 issued another executive order mandating the use of "clear language" in certain legislation and rules.

President Clinton went much further in 1998 when he issued an order not only requiring the use of "plain language" in both rules and other types of documents issued by federal agencies but establishing a framework for implementing the policy.[9] More recently, President Obama signed Executive Order 13563 in 2011 that mandated that each federal agency review its rules and "ensure that regulations are written in plain language, and easy to understand."

Although no further action was taken in the Bush Administration to advance the use of plain language by the Federal Government, in 2010, Congress passed and President Obama signed the Plain Writing Act of 2010, 5 U.S.C. § 301 note. It requires federal

---

[8] The article cited to support this claim is Lutz, *Notes Toward a Description of Doublespeak (Revised)*, 13 (n.2) Quarterly Review of Doublespeak 10-11 (January 1987). This is inaccurate. Lutz does not discuss the matter. On page 10 of the issue, which is printed in two columns, there is a note titled "Plain English Loses Again" that comes before the Lutz article. It states that "In 1972 the Nixon Administration decreed that henceforth the Federal Register was to be written in 'laymen's terms' " but with no citation. There is no such order published in the Federal Register. An inquiry to the Nixon Library by the authors received an email reply from a archivist at the library stating that she could not find any record of such an order at the library or on the website of The American Presidency Project.

[9] The history of the presidential executive orders is detailed in Berent, Plain Writing Legislative History 2007-2010, www.Plain-Writing-Association.org (2012). See also www.plainlanguage.gov, Government Mandates (2012).

agencies to use "plain writing" in government documents issued to the public and sets up procedures for implementing the requirement. While passage of the Act was hailed as a major step forward in the government's use of plain language, the Act does not apply to either statutes passed by Congress or rules issued by Federal agencies. Further, its definition of clear writing is not very strong. The Act defines it to mean "writing that is clear, concise, well-organized, and follows other best practices appropriate to the subject or field and intended audience." It is doubtful, consequently, that the Act will have much effect.

The United States Supreme Court has primary responsibility for adopting rules governing procedures in the Federal Courts.[10] It exercises that responsibility through the US Judicial Conference, which in turn acts through a Standing Committee on Rules of Practice and Procedure. For many years, it adopted rules written in traditional legal style, but in 1997, the Standing Committee adopted Guidelines for Drafting and Editing Court Rules designed to apply basic Plain English principles to the federal rules. These guidelines were first used in a revision of the Federal Rules of Appellate Procedure in 1998 and more recently in revisions of the Civil Procedure Rules in 2007 and the Federal Rules of Evidence in 2011.

At the state level, several states have adopted plain language requirements for some consumer contracts and insurance policies. None has adopted similar requirements for either statutes or rules. In Great Britain, the rules of civil procedure were rewritten in 1999 with one of the goals that they could be understood by the litigant not represented by a lawyer.

D. CRITICS OF PLAIN ENGLISH IN DRAFTING STATUTES AND RULES

Although there has been no meaningful criticism of the use of Plain English in the drafting of government communications and consumer, insurance, and other types of private legal documents, a small group of experts in the field criticize its use in the drafting of statutes and rules. One of the first was Professor Frank Grad, for many years the director of the Legislative Drafting Research Fund at Columbia University. In 1979 he wrote that "*[m]any problems that need legislative resolution are complex and difficult. . . . We need complex language to state problems of law or fact . . . . If complex problems require complex language for their resolution, so be it.*"[11]

Perhaps the best summary of the objections to Plain English (or Plain Language) is the 2003 article *Plain Language in Legislative Drafting: An Achievable Objective or a Laudable Ideal?* by Brian Hunt.[12] The author, a staff member of the Office of Parliamentary Counsel in Ireland, the drafting service for the Irish Parliament, started out the article by saying that he is "*moderately in favour of the use of plain*

---

[10] 28 U.S.C. §§ 2071-2077.

[11] Grad, *Legislative Drafting as Legal Problem Solving — Form Follows Function, in* Drafting Documents in Plain English 481, 489 (Practicing Law Institute 1979).

[12] Hunt, 24 Statute L. Rev. 112 (2003).

language in legislative drafting"[13] but then devotes the rest of the article to showing why it really does not work.

He begins by stating and then challenging the two basic assumptions of Plain English advocates. The first is that ordinary people have a desire to read legislation. He suggests there is little evidence to support the statement, but offers little evidence to refute it. The second assumption is that Plain English legislation will function as effectively as that drafted in traditional style. His argument against this assumption is that Plain English is not inherently clear because no word is inherently clear. He concludes, consequently, that using plain or simpler words in a statute produces no greater clarity than the traditional language of the law.

His only solution to the inherent lack of clarity in any word is, adopting the suggestion of Francis Bennion and Peter Blume,[14] to have each new item of legislation be accompanied by explanatory materials that will explain the changes in the law contained in it. In his and Bennion and Blume's view, lawyers are the intended audience of legislation and should be drafted with only them in mind. Communicating the meaning of legislation is an entirely different function. That should be included in explanations and summaries addressed to the general public.

It is hard to imagine a worse proposal. If words are so inherently unclear that it is a waste of time to worry about clarity in a statute, the same is true for words in an explanatory document. What is worse, if the words in a statute are interpreted to mean one thing and the words in an explanation to mean another, there is a conflict that a court will almost certainly resolve in favor of the statute, to the detriment of the person who relied on the explanation. Hunt's solution is really an argument for drafting a statute in as clear language as possible so that it can be understood by the largest audience possible, including both lawyers and the public.

Hunt also ignores the drafting techniques that are an essential part of the Plain English approach to statute and rule drafting. Word selection is only one part of Plain English. Drafting style goes hand and hand with it.

Hunt and other critics of Plain English also discuss it only in terms of statutes. Equally if not more important is its use in administrative rules. Not only are there far more rules than statutes, they are far more likely to be drafted and applied by non-lawyers, and most certainly to be applicable to and read by non-lawyers.

E. OUR VIEW

In our view, the proponents of Plain English as the cure for the historic and continuing problem of poor legal drafting, and particularly poorly drafted statutes and rules, have much the better argument. There is no excuse for a drafter of a statute or rule to use any drafting style that is not designed to make a statute or rule as clear and as understandable as possible to the general public or to use any words that are not

---

[13] *Id.*

[14] Bennion, *Don't Put the Law into Public Hands*, The Times, December 24, 1995; Blume, *The Communication of Legal Rules*, 11 Statute L. Rev. 189 (1990).

in common usage. This approach, which is known as Plain English, dates back over two hundred years but has been largely ignored by those who draft statues and rules for reasons that have no validity.

The authors have written this book in an effort to present the Plain English approach to drafting a statute or rule in a form that can be used both as a teaching tool in a law school and as a manual for use by a statute or rule drafter. We believe that the goal of lawmakers should be to have laws written in language that enables the public to understand their rights and duties under them. Following the Plain English principles and rules set out in this book will guide the drafter of a statute or rule in accomplishing that goal.

PART II

THE SPECIAL ENVIRONMENT OF DRAFTING STATUTES AND RULES

Chapter 2

HOW STATUTES GET MADE IN A LEGISLATIVE BODY

No man's life, liberty, or property is safe while the legislature is in session.[1]

A. THE DRAFTING PROCESS

If one were to attempt to describe in general terms the origins of statutes, the attempt would surely be a failure. There are almost as many sources for different statutes as there are individual bills introduced in a legislative body. The most that can be said is that every bill starts off as an idea in some individual's mind. From then on, the route to drafting a bill that incorporates the idea into a bill that is introduced into a legislative body and from there to an enacted statute has no uniform track.

The simplest and most direct track would be for a person with the idea (the proponent) to contact the person's representative in a legislative body (the sponsor) expressing the idea and requesting the representative to draft and introduce a bill to accomplish the idea. The sponsor could then request a staff member in the sponsor's personal office or on a committee on which the sponsor serves, or the bill drafting service for the legislative body of which the sponsor is a member, to draft the bill.

Far more likely, however, is for the proponent to first solicit the views and support of others, such as neighbors or members of a group or organization to which the proponent belongs. They could first attempt to get broader support from the community or affiliated organizations or simply approach the local representative directly. The bodies or organizations that are involved in the legislative process are myriad, ranging from government officers and agencies to industry and volunteer groups such as bar associations and law reformers. Many governmental bodies and public and private organizations have paid lobbyists at the local, state, and federal levels to handle taking the legislative proposals that percolate up from their members through both the drafting and enactment processes.

No matter what simple or complicated process leads up to the introduction of a bill in a legislative body, the one statement that can be made with certainty is that at some point, one person will be given the task of drafting a bill that incorporates the idea so that the sponsor can formally introduce the bill. How that bill gets drafted is, of course, the focus of this book.

---

[1] Often attributed to Mark Twain, but F. Schapiro, Yale Book of Quotations 772 (2006) says it is from an 1866 opinion by New York Surrogate Judge Gordon Tucker in the case of *Estate of AB.*

Taking an idea that calls for a statute and converting the idea into a formal bill that can become the statute is no easy task. It requires the ability to understand what idea it is that the proponent is suggesting and what its sponsor wants to accomplish. It also requires the ability to understand how to craft that idea into legislative language that will convert the idea into a statute.

The bill drafting manual for the Florida Senate accurately describes the first task of the drafter in the following terms:

> *The first step in drafting any bill is to understand what the sponsor intends to accomplish through the proposed legislation. Occasionally the initial instructions provided to the drafter will be sufficient. Often, however, they are not, and the drafter must seek clarification from the bill sponsor. After reviewing the technical and substantive issues discussed in this manual, all drafters, regardless of experience, should recognize more clearly what questions to ask. Asking the right questions is critical. A failure to communicate at the outset can result in the failure of the bill to effectuate the sponsor's intent.[2]*

Once the drafter has the basic ideas of the sponsor in mind, the drafting process can begin. The same Florida Senate drafting manual, paraphrasing one of the authors' earlier writings, describes what happens next:

> *Robert J. Martineau . . . asserts that the sponsor of legislation rarely has more than a rough idea of what his or her draft should include. Martineau explains that drafting does not merely express the ideas and intent of the sponsor which are already formed, but develops those ideas and intent as only the art of writing can. Martineau tells us that most words chosen by the drafter represent policy choices. The number and nature of choices that the sponsor or drafter must make become apparent only when drafting the proposal. The drafter must first consult with the sponsor or make a choice and bring it to the sponsor's attention, explain the options and the reasons for the choice, and follow the sponsor's will. Martineau is right! Drafting is not merely the process by which the drafter chooses words to express choices already made, but it is the process by which the drafter identifies options and makes choices.*

There is one more aspect to the process of consultation between the drafter and the legislative sponsor over available choices identified by the drafter in the drafting process that does not become apparent until well into the drafting process. It is that in many if not most cases the sponsor does not have any fixed views on what particular choice should be made. In this situation, the sponsor will either rely on the advice of the drafter or simply leave the choice up to the drafter. In either case, the drafter, by default, becomes the policy maker.

The drafter as policy maker is both an opportunity and a danger for the drafter. Obviously, if the drafter has strong ideas of what the policy should be, the drafter can incorporate those ideas into the bill. There is a great danger, however, that the drafter

---

[2] Office of Bill Drafting Services, Manual for Drafting Legislation 1-2 (6th ed., 2009).

will manipulate the consultative process with the sponsor to ensure that the drafter's policy choices are chosen or at least accepted by the sponsor. The drafter who engages in that type of manipulation is abusing the role of the drafter and thus should avoid, whenever possible, over-stepping that role.

Notwithstanding this warning, candor requires the authors to acknowledge that they have on many occasions volunteered to serve as the drafter for a committee or other group assigned the task of preparing a constitutional amendment, statute, or rule on a topic in which they have been interested. They have done this for two reasons — to ensure a well drafted proposal and to have an influence on the policy contained in the proposal. They have always recognized, however, their obligation to make the other committee members aware of their general views on policy.

The dual role of the drafter as both drafter and default policy-maker is one the authors bring to the attention of students in legislative drafting courses, both to encourage interest in the course and to show students the importance of the drafter in the legislative and rule making process.

A key factor in the drafting process and the policy development that goes with it is the drafting rules and principles contained in chapters 10-13. Following the principles and rules is the best way for the drafter to both express the intent of the sponsor and to identify the policy choices to be incorporated in the draft.

Needless to say, the drafting process does not usually end with the first draft. A bill can go through a whole series of drafts, sometimes over several years, before it is ready to be introduced. This process can be very frustrating to the drafter, especially when a policy choice once made is revisited. A policy change made later in the process can often upset the whole structure of a draft, requiring a complete revision to incorporate the policy change.

One other point is most important for the drafter — the more time spent on drafting, the clearer and more concise the draft can be. There is an old saying attributed to a variety of individuals from Winston Churchill to President Wilson: *"If you want me to give a 5 minute speech, I need two weeks to prepare, but if you want me to give an hour speech, I am ready now."*[3] The same principle applies to statute and rule drafting. A long, poorly-drafted statute or rule can be drafted in a very short time. A well-crafted one that is both clear and concise will take a very long time.

And then there is the enactment process.

B.   THE ENACTMENT PROCESS

There are two things you don't want to see being made — sausage and legislation.[4]

---

[3] www.quoteland.com, Churchill quote on speech preparation.

[4] This quote is often attributed to Otto von Bismark, German Chancellor in the late 19th century, but that attribution has been questioned. Rosenthal, *The Legislature as Sausage Factory*, State Legislatures 12-15 (September, 2001).

1. The Formal Process

The role played by a bill's drafter once it is introduced will vary from bill to bill. Depending upon circumstances, the drafter may stay with the bill through the entire process, or the drafter may never see it again. If the former, the drafter will prepare each amendment proposed by the sponsor or some other member of the legislature. When that occurs, the drafter can make sure the amendment is consistent with the rest of the bill both in substance and drafting style. If the latter, the drafter has no control over substance or style, so there is always a great risk that the drafter's carefully constructed bill can become a mishmash of substance and style for which the drafter would prefer to deny responsibility. Unfortunately, the drafter seldom has any control over which path is followed.

Whether or not the bill drafter plays any role in the enactment process, the drafter must have a basic understanding of the two processes by which a bill becomes law in Congress or a state legislature. The first is the formal legal process, established by constitutional provisions and the rules of each house of the legislature (Nebraska having the only unicameral legislature). At the very least, the drafter must know the requirements as to form (discussed in Chapter 6) and arrangement as well as substantive requirements (discussed in Chapter 7). These will determine to a major degree the structure of the bill and may have some effect on its substance.

Once introduced, most of what happens after that is set out in the rules of the house considering it. If passed in that house, the bill is sent to the other house for consideration in accordance with the second house's rules. If passed there, it is then sent to the executive for signing or veto. If the second house amends the bill in any way, it must be sent back to the first house for it to approve or reject the amended bill. If the first house does not agree to the amendments, the two variations of the bill can be sent to a conference committee composed of members of each house to work out an agreement acceptable to both houses. If both houses accept the conference committee's version, the bill goes to the executive for signing or veto. If vetoed, each house has a chance to override the veto with a super-majority, usually required in each house.

Following are diagrams that show this process for both Congress and a state legislature.

FEDERAL

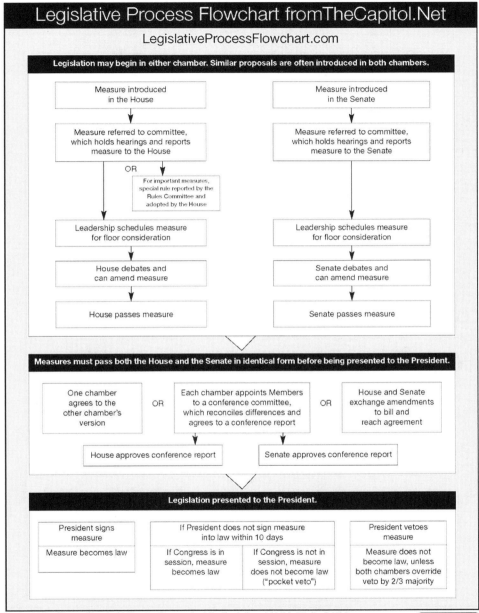

STATE

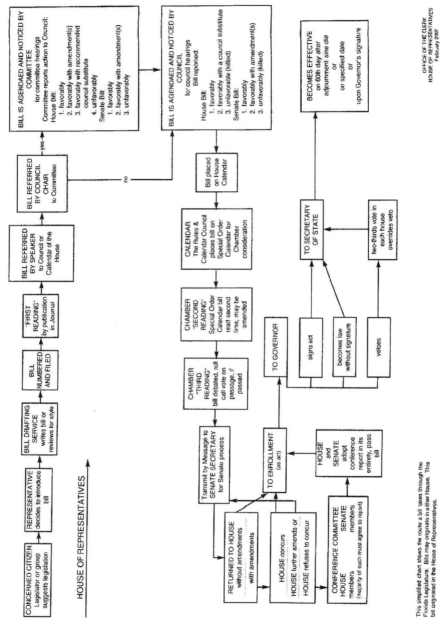

How An Idea Becomes A Law

2.   The Political Process

The second process governing the enactment of a bill is the political one. While the narrative description and these diagrams show a neat and logical process, the reality of the political process is usually quite different. The following is the history of a bill relating to condominium and homeowners association fees that was enacted into law in Florida in 2011. As can be seen, the bill was originally introduced in the House of Representatives. After consideration in several committees, the House passed and sent it to the Senate where it was considered by several committees, along with a similar bill that had been introduced in the Senate. It was a tortuous process to be sure, but one that did result in the enactment of a change in the law. Many bills can go through a similar process but never make it out of one of the committees to which it is assigned for consideration.

One thing is certain — the political process in a legislative body — federal, state, or local — is highly uncertain. There is no pattern, no one size fits all. A bill can pass in only a few days with no amendments or it can take years, with the final bill bearing no relationship to the bill originally introduced. Similarly, the role of the original drafter in the political process can be just as varied, from never seeing a bill after the original draft to drafting an amendment on the floor just before passage.

Florida Senate

CS/CS/CS/HB 1195: Condominium/Cooperative/Homeowners' Associations

> GENERAL BILL by Judiciary Committee; Economic Affairs Committee; Civil Justice Subcommittee; Moraitis; Grant; (CO-INTRODUCER) McBurney.
>
> Condominium/Cooperative/Homeowners' Associations; Revises & provides various provisions relating to specified condominium, cooperative, & homeowners' associations, including records, elections, fees, powers, duties, officers, meetings, notices, governance, foreclosure, liens, & bulk assignees & bulk buyers.
>
> **Last Action:** 06/23/2011 Chapter No. <u>2011-196</u>
>
> **Effective Date:** July 1, 2011

Bill History

DATE	CHAMBER	ACTION
03/03/2011	House	• Filed
03/08/2011	House	• Introduced — HJ 1050
3/14/2011	House	• Referred to Civil Justice Subcommittee; Insurance and Banking Subcommittee; Judiciary Committee — HJ 220
03/25/2011	House	• PCS on Committee agenda — Civil Justice Subcommittee, 03/29/11, 12:00 pm, 404 HOB
03/29/2011	House	• CS by Civil Justice Subcommittee; YEAS 13 NAYS 0 — HJ 415
04/05/2011	House	• Pending review of CS under Rule 7.19(c) • CS by Civil Justice Subcommittee read 1st time — HJ 412
04/06/2011	House	• Original reference(s) removed: Insurance and Banking Subcommittee • CS referred to Economic Affairs Committee; Judiciary Committee — HJ 450 • Now in Economic Affairs Committee — HJ 450
04/08/2011	House	• On Committee agenda — Economic Affairs Committee, 04/12/11, 1:00 pm, Reed Hall
04/12/2011	House	• CS/CS by Economic Affairs Committee; YEAS 16 NAYS 0 — HJ 619
04/13/2011	House	• Pending review of CS under Rule 7.19(c) • CS/CS by Economic Affairs Committee read 1st time — HJ 617
04/14/2011	House	• Now in Judiciary Committee — HJ 641
04/19/2011	House	• On Committee agenda — Judiciary Committee, 04/21/11, 11:00 am, 404 HOB
04/21/2011	House	• CS/CS/CS by — Judiciary Committee; YEAS 18 NAYS 0 — HJ 7760
4/25/2011	House	• Pending review of CS -under Rule 7.19(c) • CS/CS/CS by Judiciary Committee read 1st time — HJ 773
04/26/2011	House	• Placed on Calendar — HJ 836
04/27/2011	House	• Placed on Special Order Calendar, 04/29/11
04/29/2011	House	• Read 2nd time — HJ 921 • Amendment(s) adopted (541223) — HJ 922 • Read 3rd time — HJ 922 • CS passed as amended; YEAS 113 NAYS 1 — HJ 922
04/29/2011	Senate	• In Messages

DATE	CHAMBER	ACTION
05/03/2011	Senate	• Received — SJ 782 • Referred to Regulated Industries; Community Affairs; Judiciary; Budget — SJ 782 • Withdrawn from Regulated Industries; Community Affairs; Judiciary; Budget — SJ 756 • Placed on Calendar, on 2nd reading • Substituted for CS/CS/CS/SB 530 — SJ 756 • Read 2nd time — SJ 756 • Read 3rd time — J 757 • CS passed; YEAS 38 NAYS 0 — SJ 757
05/03/2011	House	• Ordered enrolled — HJ 1103
06/13/2011		• Signed by Officers and presented to Governor
06/21/2011		• Approved by Governor
06/23/2011		• Chapter No. 2011-196

Chapter 3

FEDERAL ADMINISTRATIVE AND COURT RULEMAKING

A. FEDERAL ADMINISTRATIVE RULEMAKING

1. History of Agency Rulemaking

The oldest federal agency still in existence is the Office of the Comptroller of the Currency, established in 1863.[1] Federal agency rules, however, did not begin to emerge until the late 19th century, but even then, there were few agencies and few regulations by each.[2] Federal agencies and their rules first became prevalent during the New Deal in the 1930s. Agencies such as the Federal Home Loan Bank Board, the Securities and Exchange Commission, the Federal Deposit Insurance Corporation, the National Labor Relations Board, and the Commodity Credit Corporation all came into existence during this era in an effort to overcome the effects of the Great Depression.

A second wave of regulatory agencies flourished in the late 1960s and early 1970s with the passage of a wide array of legislation to address various social issues and concerns. Congress created the Department of Transportation for transportation programs and safety and the Environmental Protection Agency to protect the environment and natural resources. The latter coincided with the passage of key environmental statutes such as the Clean Air Act and Clean Water Act in 1970. Congress also established the Occupational Safety and Health Administration within the Department of Labor to protect worker safety. There was a virtual explosion of executive branch agencies which adopted rules to implement various legislative initiatives.[3]

Prior to 1936, agencies published their own regulations in whatever manner they deemed appropriate, with little consistency in approach. The general public and affected entities had no single place to find federal regulatory requirements. There was no internet and thus no internet search capability. To address the lack of access,

---

[1] *See* Report to Congress on the Costs and Benefits of Federal Regulation, Office of Management & Budget, available at http://gerogewbush-whitehouse.archives.gov/ombinforeg/chapt1.html.

[2] *Id.* Although the Administrative Procedure Act defines "Rule" (see Section 3.a.i, below) in a manner that can encompass more than regulations adopted after notice and comment rulemaking, the terms are generally used interchangeably and are so used in this book.

[3] *Id.*

Congress passed the Federal Register Act in 1935.[4] The Act requires an agency's rules to be published in the Federal Register. Initially, an agency had to publish only final rules, but in 1946, the Administrative Procedure Act (APA) required that an agency publish a notice of a proposed rule. The further requirement to publish a preamble to the rule to explain the agency's basis and purpose of the rule became effective in 1973.

The expansion of the federal regulatory world over the last 50 years is best shown by the size of the Federal Register itself. In 1959, the Federal Register for the entire year encompassed 11,116 pages.[5] That total grew to 21,088 in 1967. In 2011, the Federal Register's number of pages was over 82,000 for the year.[6]

The Federal Register Act also required that a compilation of all existing federal regulations be compiled and periodically updated. This compilation is known as the Code of Federal Regulations (CFR). Since 1967, there has been an annual update. The first codification of all existing rules on the books was completed in 1939. It encompassed 15 volumes and over 39,000 pages. Between 1960 and 1967, the CFR grew from 60 to 110 volumes.[7] Today, the CFR is over 200 volumes, divided into 50 titles, and when stacked on a shelf takes up over 25 feet of shelf space.

2. Source of Rulemaking Authority

As a general matter, an agency can exercise only the authority a legislature has expressly given to it. The authority to issue federal rules comes from Congress in several different forms. First, Congress can provide a very general grant of authority to an agency to regulate in a specific area with little specific direction other than a broad directive to establish the rules necessary to address some specific issue, such as worker safety. Historically, this type of authority was fairly common, but is less so today.

Second, Congress can and has become more prescriptive in restricting the agency as to the substance of issues it may address in issuing rules covering particular areas. It is common process today for Congress to set forth in fairly explicit terms the types of rules (and often the timetable) for the Agency to address particular issues. For example, through the Clean Air Act Amendments of 1990, Congress directed the EPA in fairly explicit terms to take a series of prescribed actions. The changes in section 112 of the Clean Air Act between the 1977 version and the version in the 1990 Amendments are an example of the contrast between this first method and second method. Prior to 1990, Congress had directed EPA to regulate hazardous air pollutants on a risk-based approach with only general guidance and no specific timetables. In the 20 year interval between the original passage of the Clean Air Act

---

[4] 44 U.S.C. §§ 1501-1511.

[5] *See A Brief History Commemorating the 70th Anniversary of the Publication of the First Issue of the Federal Register*, Office of the Federal Register, at 10. Report available online at http://www.archives.gov/federal-register/the-federal-register/history.pdf.

[6] *Id.*

[7] *See* R. McKinney, *A Research Guide to the Federal Register and Code of Federal Regulations* (August 2010), originally published in 46 Law Library Lights 10 (2002).

in 1970 and 1990, the EPA had identified and regulated only a handful of hazardous pollutants from a small number of sources. Frustrated by that limited action, Congress was very prescriptive in the 1990 Amendments in directing EPA to issue rules to regulate hazardous air pollutant sources. Congress listed 189 pollutants in the statute and then directed the EPA to identify and list all major industrial source categories within a year. It further prescribed that within 2 years, it issue standards for at least 40 categories, 25 percent of all categories within 4 years, and all source categories within 10 years. The statute also prescribed the level of technology the EPA must use, plus numerous other very rigid requirements. Congress also specifically directed the EPA to issue regulations to address other air toxin problems such as urban air toxins, smaller area sources, and numerous other specific requirements.

A third way that an agency can undertake a rulemaking process is in response to a petition from a third party. Section 553(e) of the Administrative Procedure Act provides that an agency must afford "any interested person the right to petition for issuance, amendment, or repeal of a rule." Many statutes also contain provisions that allow a person or organization to petition an agency to commence a rulemaking process to address a problem within the general jurisdiction of the agency. If the agency does not want to undertake a rulemaking process in response to the petition, it can deny the petition. That denial is subject to judicial review.

If the adoption of a rule is discretionary for the agency, a court typically gives the agency broad deference on whether to undertake a rulemaking procedure. However, if a statute requires an agency to undertake a rulemaking process within a specified time and it fails to meet that timetable, the agency is subject to a "deadline suit" for failure to perform a nondiscretionary duty. For example, under section 304(a)(2) of the Clean Air Act, a citizen may sue to compel the EPA to perform a nondiscretionary duty by filing an action in federal district court.[8] Such an action usually results in a court ordered consent decree requiring the agency to issue a rule by a new deadline.

A fourth way Congress can direct an agency to undertake a rulemaking procedure is to order an agency to conduct a study or investigation to determine if a rule is warranted. Congress can require a report or study to be conducted on a specific problem. If the agency makes certain findings as part of that study, it may be obligated to undertake a rulemaking procedure. Again, in the 1990 CAA amendments, Congress directed the EPA to study mercury and other air toxin emissions from electric utilities and determine if it was "appropriate and necessary to regulate those emissions."

---

[8] 42 U.S.C. § 7604(a)(2); *see also Sierra Club v. Thomas*, 828 F.2d 783, 791 (D.C. Cir. 1987) (district courts have jurisdiction under C.A.A. § 304(a)(2) to enforce "date-certain" deadlines).

3. The Rulemaking Process

a. Introduction

There are various steps in a typical rulemaking process. Many of these steps are mandated under the Administrative Procedure Act (5 U.S.C. §§ 551 et seq.), the general federal statute governing rulemaking procedures. Some steps in the process discussed below are not mandated by the APA but are common steps in rulemakings today. Mandatory steps under the APA are noted. In addition to the APA, many specific statutes granting rulemaking authority to a particular agency also add additional procedural requirements. A rule drafter must always refer to the underlying grant of authority to conduct a rulemaking procedure to examine not only the scope of rulemaking authority but also to determine if it specifies any procedural requirements the agency must follow.

The federal rulemaking process has many procedural requirements imposed by statute or Executive Order. General rulemaking procedures were set forth in the APA originally enacted in 1946, but Congress and the President have added many additional procedural requirements. The APA sets forth various types of rulemaking procedures that agencies can utilize: formal, hybrid, direct final, negotiated, and informal rulemaking. Agencies develop the vast majority of agency rules using the informal rulemaking process set forth under the APA. For this reason, the "informal" rulemaking process is the focus of this chapter. Informal rulemaking is also known as notice and comment rulemaking.

This section addresses the basic steps in the informal rulemaking process. The next section addresses additional procedural requirements that apply to certain types of rules.

i. The Informal Rulemaking Process[9]

---

[9] Figure from Congressional Research Service. *See* Copeland, *The Federal Rulemaking Process: An Overview*, CRS Report RL 32240 at 2.

* The Office of Management and Budget's (OMB) office of Information and Regulatory Affairs (OIRA) reviews only significant rules, and does not review any rules submitted by independent regulatory agencies.

The initial question is what is a *"rule"*? The APA defines a *"rule"* as follows:

the whole or a part of an agency statement of general or particular applicability and future effect designed to implement, interpret, or prescribe law or policy or describing the organization, procedure, or practice requirements of an agency and includes the approval or prescription for the future of rates, wages, corporate or financial structures or reorganizations thereof, prices, facilities, appliances, services or allowances therefor or of valuations, costs, or accounting, or practices bearing on any of the foregoing.[10]

ii. Commencing the Rulemaking Process — Advanced Notice of Proposed Rulemaking

An agency often uses the advance notice of proposed rulemaking (ANPR) to seek early comment from the public before it formalizes its position into a proposed rule. The ANPR is not a mandatory step under the Administrative Procedure Act. It is entirely up to an agency to decide if it wants to issue an ANPR. The procedure is often used to solicit a broad range of suggestions and ideas and collect additional information to help an agency formulate a proposed rule. As discussed in more detail below, courts have held that a final rule must be a "logical outgrowth" of a proposed rule. This limitation typically means that a proposed rule represents a substantially refined position of what the agency wants to include in the final rule. However, if the agency wants to seek comment and suggestions before developing a proposed rule, it can use the ANPR as a way to lay out a broad range of options — or no specific options — without meeting all the APA requirements for a fully developed proposed rule.

The ANPR can be a particularly useful tool on a controversial rulemaking subject to elicit a range of opinion and content of the proposed rule. The ANPR also acts as a way to bring forth technical information which may be of assistance to the agency as it develops its rule and address the many problems addressed in the rule. The ANPR is published in the Federal Register. The downside of the ANPR is, of course, that it adds another step in the process and can lengthen the time to complete the entire process.

iii. Preparation of the Proposed Rule

Section 553 of the Administrative Procedure Act, (5 U.S.C. § 553) sets forth the general procedures that govern agency rulemaking. The section's notice provisions do not apply to interpretative rules, general statements of policy, or rules of internal practices or procedure of an agency. Under the section, an agency must publish a notice of proposed rulemaking in the Federal Register and provide at a minimum: (a) a statement of the time, place and nature of the public rulemaking proceedings; (b) the legal authority under which the rule is proposed; and (c) either the terms of the substance of the proposed rule or a description of the subjects and issues involved. The agency must also provide a process for interested persons to participate in

---

[10] 5 U.S.C. § 551(4).

rulemaking through public hearings, submission of written data or comments, and other information. With the advent of internet access, one of the primary means for submitting comments is via the "edocket" (www.regulations.gov/) established by the Office of the Federal Register. Indeed, Congress requires an agency to provide for electronic submissions. The edocket also provides almost immediate access by parties to comments filed by others electronically.

The Federal Register office requires that each proposed rule preamble set forth the information under certain prescribed headings: (1) Agency; (2) Action; (3) Summary; (4) Dates; (5) Addresses; (6) For Further Information Contact; and (7) Supplementary Information. An agency must include each section and in that order.

The "Agency" section simply identifies the agency issuing the proposed rule. The "Action" section identifies the action as a proposed rule (as opposed to a final rule), general statement of policy, or other action.

In the "Summary" section, the Agency gives a brief overview of the problems it seeks to address, the actions under consideration, and the basic rationale for the rule being proposed. The summary will explain what action is being taken, why it is necessary, and the projected impact of the rule.

In the "Dates," "Addresses," and "For Further Information" sections of the preamble, the agency formally seeks comments and explains how to file comments, and whom to contact if the reader has questions or needs additional information.

The "Supplementary Information" section is where the drafter explains the proposed rule in detail. This section will also contain the technical or other supporting information in the docket relied upon in developing the proposal. The section will also summarize the legal authority on which the rule is based. It must explain clearly who will be affected by the proposed rule and projected costs or other effects. This section of the preamble will also explain how the agency has complied with other procedural requirements such as the statutory provisions and executive orders discussed below. If the agency wants comment on specific detailed issues, it can solicit it in this section of the preamble.

Following the preamble, the Federal Register notice will set forth the text of the rule being proposed.

iv.   Preparation of the Final Rule

Following publication of the notice of proposed rulemaking, the official public comment period will open for public comment. The APA requires for the final rule that the agency provide a concise general statement of the basis and purpose of the rule. The Supreme Court has explained this requirement as follows:

> *The agency must examine the relevant data and articulate a satisfactory explanation of its action, including a "rational connection between the facts and the choice made."*[11]

---

[11] *Motor Vehicle Manufacturers' Ass'n v. State Farm Mutual Automobile Ins. Co.*, 463 U.S. 29, 43, 103

The agency must also ensure that the final rule is a logical outgrowth of the proposal. Otherwise, a court may find that the agency did not provide adequate public notice in the proposal of the scope of the rule. A rule is not effective until at least 30 days after publication in the Federal Register, except when (1) the rule grants or recognizes and exemption or relieves a restriction, (2) it is a general statement of policy or an interpretative rule, or (3) the agency demonstrates good cause for not doing so.

The agency will prepare its proposed final rule after reviewing the comments provided during the public comment process. Once it prepares a proposed final rule and preamble, if the rule is significant it must go back to the Office of Information and Regulatory Affairs ("OIRA"), a part of the Office of Management and Budget ("OMB"), for review in accordance with EO 12866, as discussed below.

In the modern administrative state, the preamble to the final rule often takes on a life of its own that is almost as important as the rule language itself. The preamble will explain the "what" and "why" of the rule and what the rule is intended to do. The preamble should explain the legal basis for the rule, whether the rule is an amendment to existing rules or a new rule, and provide a summary of the underlying data and facts relied upon by the agency in drafting the rule. The preamble should also summarize important requirements of the rule and timetables for complying with the rule. It can also explain alternatives considered in the rulemaking process.

If a rule is challenged, a reviewing court will examine the preamble in detail to determine if the agency provided a sufficient explanation of the rule, the intended effect of the action, how the rule relates to the underlying statute, and how the agency's action is reasonable and consistent with the underlying statutory directives. The agency will also explain in the preamble how the agency has complied with all necessary procedural requirements, such as the various other procedural requirements discussed below.

A court typically will require an agency to respond to significant comments made during the comment period and explain why the comment was accepted or rejected. Although not required under the APA provisions, some statutes specifically impose the duty to respond to comments in the statute itself.[12] A statute may also contain additional procedural requirements beyond the APA, including a more detailed explanation of the rule in the preamble, or a more extensive record to support the rule.[13]

v.   Exemptions from Informal Rulemaking Requirements

Section 553 of the APA includes several exemptions from the procedural requirements. Some types of rules are totally exempt, including rules addressing: (1) military or foreign affairs functions of the United States; (2) agency management or

---

S. Ct. 2856, 2866 (1983), *quoting Burlington Truck Lines v. United States*, 371 U.S. 156, 168, 83 S. Ct. 239, 245-46 (1962).

[12] *See, e.g.*, the Clean Air Act procedural requirements in 42 U.S.C. § 7607(d)(B)(6).

[13] *See, e.g.*, procedural requirements set forth in the Toxic Substances Control Act, 15 U.S.C. §§ 2670, 2058, and the Clean Air Act, 42 U.S.C. § 7607(d).

personnel; or (3) public property, loans, grant, benefits or contracts.[14] In addition, rules of agency organization and practice or procedure are exempt from the APA notice and comments requirements, but they must be intra-agency type requirements, not ones that impose obligations or burdens on others. The APA requirements also do not apply to interpretive rules or general statements of policy. All of these types of rules are considered non-legislative rules because they do not create any new duties on third parties, but only clarify or interpret already existing rules or interpret a statute. If a rule has a substantive effect on third parties, it is considered a legislative rule. Legislative rules are subject to the APA procedural requirements.

Much controversy has surrounded agency use of guidance or policy or interpretative rules. In many cases, affected parties have argued that the agency has created new substantive obligations or changed longstanding positions via guidance or interpretative rules that were not subject to public notice and comment. Similarly, agencies will offer policy guidance as non-binding, but then treat the guidance as if it were a binding rule and hold parties to it. Affected parties routinely challenge agency policies as unlawful rulemakings.

Section 553 also contains a "good cause" exception provision to allow an agency to avoid the notice and comment rulemaking procedure under certain limited exceptions. To use the good cause exception, section 553(b)(B) requires the agency to show that the use of the full procedures are "impracticable, unnecessary, or contrary to the public interest." The exceptions for good cause are to be narrowly construed, and the burden is on the agency to justify dispensing with the notice and comment procedures.

4. Statutory Constraints on The Rulemaking Process

Numerous statutory provisions impose substantive and procedural requirements on an agency in adopting a rule. First, as noted above, the general authority to issue a rule by an agency must come from some statutory grant of authority. Second, the statute that creates the agency or other statutes that direct the agency to issue certain types of rules or grant them the discretion to do so will specify the substantive requirements that the agency must address. The directives in these statutes can be general or very detailed.

There are several different provisions of environmental statutes that direct the EPA to issue certain types of rules, or grant it the authority to do so. For example, section 112 of the Clean Air Act[15] directs the EPA to establish standards for hazardous air pollutants. This single statutory provision contains numerous specific rulemaking directives. Section 112(d) sets forth the substantive requirements on what the EPA must include in the rule. A statutory provision can be very specific, as in the case of mandatory language, or it can be a more general direction to the agency to address certain topics.

---

[14] 5 U.S.C. § 553(a).

[15] 42 U.S.C. § 7412.

The APA's procedural requirements and the requirements of the specific statute that authorizes an agency to issue rules are not the only requirements imposed upon agencies in the federal administrative rulemaking process. Others are:

a. Congressional Review

Although an agency may only act when it has authority delegated by Congress, the legislature also has an oversight role on an agency at the end of the rulemaking process. The Congressional Review Act[16] was enacted as part of the Small Business Regulatory Enforcement Fairness Act of 1996. The law provides that before a rule can take effect, the promulgating agency must submit a report on the rule which includes a copy of the rule to each house of Congress and to the General Accounting Office prior to publication of the rule in the Federal Register. A major rule may not take effect until at least 60 days after publication. If the rule is a "major rule" (over $100 million in impact), special procedural requirements apply and the GAO will determine if those procedures were followed. Within 60 days after Congress receives an agency's rule, a member of Congress can introduce a resolution to disapprove the rule. If the resolution to disapprove the rule is passed by both houses of Congress, it nullifies the rule.

If Congress does disapprove a rule, the agency may not adopt a substantially similar rule without additional statutory authorization. While this sounds like it would lead to an endless stream of resolutions of disapproval and constantly jeopardize agency action, the reality is that of the more than 50,000 rules submitted to the GAO since 1996, only one has been overturned under this process — the ergonomics rule in 2001.[17]

b. Paperwork Reduction

The Paperwork Reduction Act[18] ("PRA") requires the adopting agency to address additional paperwork burdens the rule may impose. OMB must approve the information collection requirements of the rule before it is effective. The rules implementing the Paperwork Reduction Act are set out at 5 C.F.R. 1320. The original PRA also established the Office of Information and Regulatory Affairs (OIRA) within the Office of Management and Budget. This Office is a clearinghouse through which a rule must pass before an agency may propose or adopt it. The Office also must approve information collection requests by an agency before it can implement the rule.

---

[16] 5 U.S.C. §§ 801 et seq.

[17] For a discussion of this action, see M. Rosenberg, *Congressional Review of Agency Rulemaking: An Update and Assessment of the Congressional Review Act after a Decade*, Congressional Research Service Report, Report RL30116, (Updated May 8,2008) at CRS-14-15. Rosenberg notes that the ergonomics rule had been a controversial rule throughout its rulemaking process and was adopted near the end of one Administration and concludes that overturning of the rule was the "product of an unusual confluence of events: control of both Houses of Congress and the presidency by the same party, the longstanding opposition by these political actors, as well as by broad components of the industry to be regulated, to the ergonomics standard, and the willingness and encouragement of a President seeking to undo a contentious, end of term rule from a previous Administration." *Id.* at CRS-15.

[18] 44 U.S.C. §§ 3501-3520.

An information request can be a part of a rule itself. Often a request is also a critical step for an agency beginning a rulemaking procedure to collect data — typically from the entities that may be subject to the rule. Under the PRA, the agency is required to publish a notice in the Federal Register that it is seeking approval of an information collection request from OMB; thus the public has an opportunity to comment on the proposed request, creating yet another administrative hurdle in the rulemaking process for an agency.

c.   Plain English

On October 13, 2010, President Obama signed into law the Plain Writing Act of 2010, which is designed to help foster "clear Government communication that the public can understand and use."[19] The Act covers a document necessary for obtaining a federal government benefit or service, or that provides information about any federal benefit or service, or that that explains how to comply with a requirement the federal government administers. The Act required agencies to begin complying with it by October, 2011. OMB has promulgated guidance for agencies on implementing Plain English principles.[20] An agency must maintain a Plain English section on its website. Several Executive Orders governing rulemaking also require rules to be written in plain English.[21]

d.   Small Business Impacts

The Regulatory Flexibility Act[22] ("RFA") requires an agency to prepare a regulatory flexibility analysis of a rule subject to notice and comment rulemaking requirements under section 553 of the APA or other statute. An agency can avoid the requirement if the agency certifies that the rule will not have an adverse impact on a substantial number of small entities such as small governmental jurisdictions or small businesses as defined by the Small Business Administration. The RFA allows judicial review of both the regulatory flexibility analysis and the certification that the rule would not have an impact on small entities.

In 1996, as part of the Small Business Regulatory Enforcement Fairness Act ("SBREFA"),[23] Congress amended the RFA to add requirements for OSHA and the EPA when either develops a rule that has direct impact on small entities. Either agency must convene a panel to review the regulatory flexibility analysis. SBREFA also added procedural requirements for a rule that affects small entities, including requiring the agency to prepare a compliance guide and to waive civil penalties in certain instances.

---

[19] Plain Writing Act of 2010, P.L. 111-274, 124 Stat. 2861, 5 U.S.C. § 301 note.

[20] See information on Plain English requirements at http://www.plainlanguage.gov/plLaw/index.cfm.

[21] *See, e.g.*, Executive Order 13563, 76 Fed. Reg. 3821 (January 21, 2011). The regulatory system "must ensure that regulations are accessible, consistent, written in plain language, and easy to understand."

[22] 5 U.S.C. §§ 601-612.

[23] P.L. 104-121 (1996).

e. Unfunded Mandates

The Unfunded Mandates Reform Act[24] was enacted to avoid imposing an unfunded mandate on a state or local government or the private sector. Under the Act, an agency that proposes a rule that includes a federal mandate that may result in the expenditure of $100 million or more in any year, must do a cost benefit assessment of the rule, provide a description of its macroeconomic effects, and address how the agency will deal with the concerns of the economic impact on state, local, or private entities. The Act also requires the agency to consult with state and local governments to provide timely comment on the proposed rule.

f. Information Quality

In 2001, Congress amended the Paperwork Reduction Act[25] adding provisions known as the Information Quality Act. This amendment was intended to ensure that information relied upon by a federal agency to support its rulemakings is quality information that can be relied on. Under the Act, each agency was to establish administrative procedures to enable a person to correct information maintained and distributed by the agency. This process can be helpful to ensure that information is accurate if an agency is releasing information about such things as how many emissions a particular source emits to the environment. But on more general information, as a practical matter, particularly in areas of scientific debate or analysis, what constitutes "quality" information may be a difficult thing to determine.

g. Environmental Impacts

The National Environmental Policy Act[26] (NEPA) was the first major environmental statute of the modern environmental protection era. NEPA requires an agency to determine whether a major federal action such as an agency rule will have a significant impact on the quality of human health or the environment. Under NEPA, if the Council on Environmental Quality determines an agency action will have no significant impact, the action may proceed. However, if it finds that there may be a significant impact, it may require the agency to prepare a full environmental impact statement.[27]

---

[24] 2 U.S.C. §§ 1501 et seq.

[25] The language was added to the Paperwork Reduction Act by section 515 of the Treasury and General Government Appropriations Act for Fiscal Year 2001. The implementing guidelines for the IQA requirements are set out by OMB in *Guidelines for Ensuring and Maximizing the Quality, Objectivity, Utility, and Integrity of Information Disseminated by Federal Agencies: Republication*, 67 Fed. Reg. 8452 (February 22, 2002).

[26] 42 U.S.C. §§ 4321-4347.

[27] NEPA's implementing regulations are set forth at 40 C.F.R. Part 1500. The NEPA process can be timing consuming and significantly impact the rulemaking process if deemed to be applicable. In addition, most agencies will have their own NEPA regulations.

5.   Executive Orders and Rulemaking Procedures

Over the years, Presidents have issued various executive orders imposing additional analysis and procedural constraints on rulemaking activities of executive branch agencies, including independent agencies. These executive orders require a variety of consultation efforts and information gathering as part of the rulemaking process. Some of the requirements have broad-based applicability to rulemaking; others are narrower, applying to only certain types of rules, or when a rule affects a specific group.

a.   Cost vs. Benefit

Executive Order 12866,[28] issued by President Clinton in 1993, requires that a regulatory action that raises a "novel legal or policy" issue, or has a $100 million impact or more is a significant regulatory action and the agency must submit it to the Office of Management and Budget (OMB) for review. OMB evaluates the agency's regulatory action to determine if the cost of the regulation is outweighed by the benefits. The agency must also evaluate alternatives to the regulatory approach contemplated. An agency rule subject to this requirement must undergo a cost-benefit analysis during the rulemaking process before it will be approved by OMB for final issuance. In January 2011, President Obama issued Executive Order 13563 in response to the anti-regulatory sentiment evident in the Congressional elections of 2010.[29] This EO reaffirms and builds on the principles of EO 12866, but goes further in its requirements to look at innovation and flexible approaches to regulations. It also directs agencies to continue to look at ways to enhance public participation. EO 13563 also directs agencies to do a retrospective review of existing rules and determine if any existing rules are obsolete, outdated, or otherwise could be modified or streamlined. In submitting a rule to OMB under EO 12866, each agency must certify that it has met the requirements of EO 12866.

b.   Tribal Consultation

Executive Order 13175[30] provides that when an agency is developing a rule that has implications for tribal governments, the agency must engage in a coordination and consultation process as part of the rulemaking process.

c.   Energy Supply Implications

In 2001, President Bush signed Executive Order 13211.[31] It requires that federal agencies submit a "Statement of Energy Effects" for an action OMB identifies as a significant energy action or that would otherwise have to be submitted to OMB as a significant regulatory action.

---

[28] 58 Fed. Reg. 51,735 (Oct. 4, 1993).

[29] 76 Fed. Reg. 3,821 (Jan. 21, 2011).

[30] 65 Fed. Reg. 67,249 (Nov. 9, 2000).

[31] 66 Fed. Reg. 28,355 (May 22, 2001).

d. Federalism

To address the constitutional principles that the federal government is one of enumerated powers and that those powers not enumerated are to be reserved to the states, Executive Order 13132[32] requires a federal agency to consider whether action is necessary at the federal level or whether it is more appropriate to be left to the states, and to engage in a consultation process when adopting a rule that may have an impact on state governments or when the agency intends to preempt state authority. In submitting a rule to OMB under 12866, the agency must demonstrate that it has complied with the federalism order and consulted with the states.

e. Children and Environmental Health Risks

For a major regulatory action that has a significant economic impact under EO 12866 and concerns an environmental health risk or safety risk that an agency has reason to believe may disproportionately affect children, EO 13045[33] requires an agency to evaluate the environmental health or safety effect of the proposed action. It must provide an explanation of why the planned regulation is preferable to other potentially effective and reasonably feasible alternatives considered by the agency.

f. Environmental Justice

In 1994, President Clinton issued Executive Order 12898[34] directing that agencies, to the greatest extent practicable and permitted by law, to make environmental justice a part of their mission. An agency must identify and address as appropriate, disproportionately high and adverse human health or environmental effects of their programs, policies, and activities on minority and low income populations.

g. Property Rights and Takings

Executive Order 12630[35], entitled "Governmental Actions and Interference with Constitutionally Protected Property Rights," gives guidance on rules that interfere with property rights. The EO directs that private property should be taken only for "real and substantial threats" and that the taking be no more than absolutely necessary.

6. Judicial Review of Agency Rulemakings

An agency rule carries a presumption that it is subject to judicial review. The APA's judicial review provisions are set forth at 5 U.S.C. §§ 701-708. Unless a statute precludes judicial review or an agency action is specifically committed to agency discretion by law, those affected by a rule may seek judicial review. The scope of review may be defined by a specific statute. If not otherwise stated, under the APA,

---

[32] 64 Fed. Reg. 43,255 (Aug. 10, 1999).

[33] 62 Fed. Reg. 19,885 (April 23, 1997).

[34] 59 Fed. Reg. 7,629 (Feb. 16, 1994).

[35] 53 Fed. Reg. 8,859 (March 18, 1988).

the reviewing court must hold unlawful and set aside any agency action, finding, or conclusion it finds to be (A) arbitrary, capricious, an abuse of discretion, or otherwise not in accordance with the law; (B) contrary to constitutional right, power, privilege or immunity; (C) in excess of statutory jurisdiction, authority, or limitations or short of statutory right; or (D) not complying with required procedures.[36]

To seek judicial review, a party must show that it is aggrieved by the agency action, has standing to seek review, and that the agency action is a final action and ripe for review. In some cases, a statute may require administrative remedies be exhausted before seeking judicial review.

Courts will afford several levels of deference to an agency in judicial review of agency rulemakings. The amount of deference depends on whether the statutory language is explicit or whether the agency is afforded broad discretion to implement congressional delegations of authority.

The seminal Supreme Court case for scope of agency discretion in interpreting a statute is *Chevron USA, Inc v. Natural Resources Defense Council*.[37] More recently in *Mead v. United States*, the Court has stated

> *that administrative implementation of a particular statutory provision qualifies for* Chevron *deference when it appears that Congress delegated authority to the agency generally to make rules carrying the force of law, and that the agency interpretation claiming deference was promulgated in the exercise of that authority.*[38]

In the same opinion, however, the Court also concluded that the level of deference will vary depending on various circumstances, including the context of the agency action, but that it is not a question of whether to defer or not.[39]

Courts tend to grant greater levels of deference to agencies on issues of highly technical or scientific nature within the purview of the agency's expertise. The Supreme Court has stated, however, that it will take a hard look at the agency decision even in areas where the agency is afforded a great degree of deference. In a seminal case involving seat belt restraints, the Supreme Court articulated the standard as follows:

> *Normally, an agency rule would be arbitrary and capricious if the agency has relied on factors which Congress has not intended it to consider, entirely failed to consider an important aspect of the problem, offered an explanation for its decision that runs counter to the evidence before the agency, or is so implausible that it could not be ascribed to a difference in view or the product of agency expertise.*[40]

---

[36] 5 U.S.C. § 706.

[37] 467 U.S. 837 (1984).

[38] 533 U.S. 218, 226-27 (2001).

[39] *Id.* at 237-38.

[40] *Motor Vehicle Manufacturers Ass'n v. State Farm Mutual Automobile Insurance Co.*, 463 U.S. 29, 43 (1983).

B. FEDERAL COURT RULES

Prior to 1938, there was no national rulemaking process for the federal courts. Each district and circuit court adopted its own rules, largely based on the rules in effect in the state in which the court was located. All of this changed beginning in 1934 with the enactment of the Rules Enabling Act[41] following a campaign for national rules by the American Bar Association.

This Act gave power to the United States Supreme Court for the first time to adopt "rules of pleading and practice" for all federal courts subject to control by Congress. The Court appointed an advisory committee that proposed rules of civil procedure which the Court adopted in 1938.

Over the years, Congress has expanded the areas in which the Court could adopt rules and the process by which it does so. Currently, there are five advisory committees that develop rules of civil, criminal, bankruptcy, appellate, and admiralty procedure and evidence. After a substantial period of public notice and consultation, the Standing Committee presents the rules to the Judicial Conference. If it approves, it submits the rules to the Supreme Court for final adoption. Congress still retains the right to amend or repeal a rule, but seldom does so.

Federal courts of appeals and district courts can adopt local rules as they always have, but only in conformity with the national rules. To ensure conformity, the circuit judicial council and the Standing Committee can review and amend or reject a local rule. The present process also requires local advisory committees and public notice and comment.

There are no national rules governing admission to the bar or discipline of lawyers. Courts of appeals and district courts each admit lawyers to practice before them mainly on the basis of admission to practice in a state. The federal courts also turn over discipline matters to the state where the lawyer is admitted.

The federal Standing Committee on rules for many years ignored the problem of the clarity with which the federal rules were drafted. They and its advisory committees used law professors who were experts in the substantive fields covered by the rules to draft them. Inevitably, the rules lacked the clarity they should have had. To overcome these deficiencies, the Standing Committee has a subcommittee on Style. In 1997, it adopted Guidelines for Drafting and Editing Court Rules, prepared by Professor Bryan A. Garner. The result has been a substantial improvement in the clarity of the federal rules. As noted in Chapter 1[C], the federal rules on appellate procedure, civil procedure, and evidence have been completely revised in the past decade to incorporate Plain English principles. The revision process is gradually being applied to all federal rules.

---

[41] Currently found in 28 U.S.C. §§ 2071-2077.

Chapter 4

STATE RULEMAKING

A. ADMINISTRATIVE RULEMAKING

1. Introduction

While federal agencies follow largely the same procedural steps and requirements for agency rulemaking, subject to specific statutory exceptions, the rulemaking process at the state level can vary widely. This chapter focuses on the rulemaking provisions of the 2010 Model State Administrative Procedure Act (Model Act or MSAPA) as a generic way to address state rulemaking procedures. Most of the provisions of the model act are taken from or modeled after one or more state statutes The rule drafter in a particular state must pay particular attention to the special procedural requirements of that state.

State rulemaking procedures typically differ from the federal rulemaking process in several key ways. First, in many states, there are commissions or boards which technically act as the "agency" for the purpose of proposing and promulgating regulations. Although most states have cabinet level departments or agencies similar to federal agencies (e.g. department of labor, environmental protection agencies, departments of revenue or commerce, health and human service agencies), many states have part-time citizen boards, who oversee the activities of those state agencies and act as a check on the rulemaking process. These boards or commissions often must approve a proposed rule before it is sent out for public comment. Likewise, the board or commission must adopt a rule before it becomes effective. These boards or commissions act as a check on the power of the executive branch agency to issue rules.

Second, in many states, after an agency has adopted a rule, it must go to a state legislative body for approval before it can become effective. The legislative oversight is yet another check on the authority of the executive branch agency. As discussed in the chapter on federal regulations, the Congressional Review Act at the federal level gives Congress some oversight of federal agencies, although as a practical matter, it is rarely exercised. At the state level, however, the legislative review process is a more routine part of the rulemaking process.

Third, in some states, there is a formal or informal added review at the gubernatorial level as a way to keep more control on executive branch agencies. The process is similar to OMB's review of agency rules at the federal level, but in many states, boards or commissions are actual rulemaking agencies, although executive branch staffs in the agencies do the actual work on rules.

2. The Model State Administrative Procedure Act

a. Introduction

The Model Act was developed by the National Conference of Commissioners of Uniform State Laws (Commission).[1] The first model act was developed in 1946 at the same time as the federal APA. It was revised in 1961 and 1981, the latter having been adopted in 8 states. The latest version of the Model Act was adopted by the Commission in July 2010, but no state has yet enacted it.

The 2010 Act is divided into the following key sections related to rulemaking: (1) general provisions; (2) public access to agency law; (3) rulemaking procedural requirements; (4) judicial review; (5) administrative hearings; and (6) rules review. The primary focus of this chapter will be on rulemaking procedures, but each of the other sections will be discussed briefly as they relate to the rulemaking process. The focus is on notice and comment type rulemaking. Provisions discussing contested cases and other adjudicatory hearing provisions of the Model Act are not addressed.

b. General Provisions

Article I of the Act includes the key definitions used in the Act. A "rule" is defined as "the whole or part of an agency statement of general applicability that implements, interprets, or prescribes law or policy or the organization, procedure, or practice requirements of an agency and has the force of law."[2] Like the federal APA, the Model Act excludes from the definition of a rule, general statements of internal management of an agency that do not affect the public, interagency memoranda or directives that do not affect private rights, opinions of a state attorney general, agency forms to implement policy, and enforcement guidelines if disclosure of such criteria would give improper advantage to persons in adverse position to the state.[3]

An "agency action" is defined as: (1) the whole or part of an order or rule; (2) the failure to issue and order or rule; or (3) an agency's performing or failing to perform a duty, function, or activity or to make a determination required by law.[4] The definition of "agency action" is important because it defines what actions are subject to judicial review.

c. Public Access to Agency Law and Policy

Article 2 of the Model Act dictates how an agency is to ensure that the public has notice of proposed and final agency actions. Section 201 directs the state entity in charge of publications to maintain an electronic record of agency actions and to publish

---

[1] The Commission is also referred to as the Uniform Law Commission (ULC). ULC members must be lawyers. It includes practitioners as well as legislators, academics, judges and legislative staff.

[2] MSAPA § 102(30). For information on the status of enactment and for an annotated version of the model act, go to http://www.nccusl.org/Act.aspx?title=State%20Administrative%20Procedure%20Act,%20Revised%20Model.

[3] *Id.*

[4] MSAPA § 102(4).

proposed and final actions in a state bulletin like the Federal Register.[5] A state bulletin should be published at least once per month. A state entity is also directed to maintain an official record of the rulemaking including the text of the rule and any supporting documents. This 2010 version of the Model Act reflects the emerging world of the internet and electronic records. The state is directed to maintain an internet site that is to include the regulations, any relevant guidance, and an electronic version of the rulemaking bulletin. The definitions of "electronic record" and "internet website" are new in the 2010 Act, as well as requirements to use internet websites for publication of rulemaking notices and related information.[6]

Section 202 of the Model Act establishes the duties of the rulemaking agency with respect to public access to or dissemination of key agency information.[7] Section 202(a) requires agencies to publish on the agency website key agency actions including the following: notices of proposed rules, final rules, regulatory analysis supporting a rule, guidance documents, final orders as well as indices of those declaratory orders and guidance documents. Documents are also to be made available through regular mail upon request.[8] Agencies may charge a reasonable fee for such requests.

To assist interested persons in understanding the procedural requirements for permit applicants, how the rulemaking process works, and other aspects of how an agency works, the Model Act also directs the agency to publish on its website all public procedures followed by the agency. The concept is to explain in simple terms how someone can apply for and get a permit or undertake some other interaction with the state agency. The more information available on the website clearly explaining the procedural requirements, the more informed a stakeholder can be when interacting with the department when commenting on a proposed rule, seeking a license or permit, or challenging a final agency action.[9] The Model Act also directs that an agency maintain a docket of ongoing rulemakings and to adopt rules for the conduct of public hearings.

d. Rulemaking Proceedings: Procedural Requirements

Article 3 sets out the Act's procedural requirements for rulemaking proceedings. The various provisions of the Model Act are similar in many ways to the procedural safeguards in the federal Administrative Procedure Act and have come from or been adopted by various states in whole or part.

---

[5] The Model Act refers to a "publisher" as the entity within the state government that is responsible for publications of the state as opposed to each regulatory entity. Who does this in each state varies. In Tennessee, for example, the publications of the official rules and the administrative bulletin known as the Tennessee Administrative Register fall within the purview of the Secretary of State's office.

[6] See MSAPA, section 102(9) ("electronic record" definition); and section 102(17) ("internet website" definition).

[7] MSAPA, section 202 (a).

[8] Id., at section 202(b).

[9] MSAPA, section 203.

i.   Introduction

The Model Act requires the creation of a rulemaking docket for all pending rulemakings that is indexed by topic. The docket is to include basic summary information about the rule, including: the subject matter of the rule, notices related to the rule, method and time for comment, how comments of others can be accessed, and information pertaining a public hearing or how to request one and the anticipated timetable for the rulemaking action.[10]

The requirement to compile a rulemaking record is becoming a more common requirement in some states and is also included in the Model Act. The purpose of a rulemaking record is to ensure that the basis for the proposed rule is provided to the public. In theory, if all parties have the same information available, the comments and agency response will be better. Likewise, if an agency rule is subject to challenge, it will be easier for a reviewing body to determine whether the agency's action was rational if the record shows the basis for the decision. If exempt under state open records laws, privileged material or certain confidential information may be precluded from the rulemaking record.[11]

ii.   Commencing the Rulemaking Process — Advanced Notice of Proposed Rulemaking

An agency often uses the advance notice of proposed rulemaking (ANPR) process to seek early comment from the public before it formalizes its position into an actual proposed rule. The ANPR is not a mandatory step under the model act; it is entirely up to an agency to decide if it wants to issue an ANPR.[12] The ANPR solicits a broad range of suggestions and ideas and collect additional information to help an agency formulate the proposed rule. Courts have held that final rules must be a "logical outgrowth" of a proposed rule. This limitation typically means that a proposed rule represents a fairly well refined position of where the agency wants to end up in the final rule. However, if it wants to seek comment and input before developing a proposed rule, it can use the ANPR as a way to lay out a broad range of options — or no specific options — without meeting all the requirements for an actual proposed rule.

The ANPR can be a useful tool on particularly controversial rulemaking subjects to elicit the range of opinion and issues that the rule will cover. The ANPR also acts as a way to develop technical information which may be of assistance to the agency as it develops the rule.

---

[10] MSAPA § 301. This section is modeled after the Minnesota provisions. M.S.A. § 14.366.

[11] A number of states have requirements for rulemaking records. *See, e.g.*, A.R.S. § 41-1029 (Arizona); C.R.S.A. § 24-4-103 (Colorado); M.S.A. § 14.365 (Minnesota); R.C.W.A. Ann. § 25-43-110 (Washington).

[12] MSAPA § 303(a).

iii.   Notice of Proposed Rulemaking

A key component of the rulemaking process is the notice of proposed rulemaking. It provides the public with notice not only of the proposed agency action but also the rationale for the action. The notice requirements of the Model Act are contained in section 304. It requires an agency to publish notice of the proposed rule at least 30 days before adoption. The notice must include the following information about the proposed rule: (i) a short explanation of the rule; (ii) a reference to the legal authority to issue the rule; (iii) the text of the proposed rule; (iv) a summary of and how a copy of the full regulatory analysis underlying the rule may be obtained; (v) how a person may comment on the rule; and (vi) citation to and summary of any technical report used in support of the rule and how to obtain a copy of the full report.[13] This language is similar in many ways to the federal requirements, although with some additional detail such as including a summary of technical report.

The agency must publish a notice in the state publication comparable to the Federal Register if the state has one. The section also requires the agency to give individual notice of a proposed rule within 3 days of publication of the notice to anyone who has requested a mailed or electronic copy of the rule.[14]

The regulatory analysis required to accompany the notice is to include an analysis of the costs and benefits of the range of alternatives within the scope of the proposed rule and a determination of whether the benefits outweigh the costs of the rule. The regulatory analysis must also demonstrate how the proposed rule will achieve the outcome of the underlying statute in a more cost effective manner than other alternatives.[15] The regulatory analysis is intended to apply only to certain rules above certain economic significance threshold, although what that level is should be is not defined in the Model Act. If the state has a reviewing body such as OMB on the federal level, the section requires the Agency to submit the regulatory analysis to that body for review.

The 30 day notice is to ensure at least some opportunity for public participation once the proposed rule is announced. The Model Act does not require a public hearing to take comment, but if it does hold a public hearing, it may be no sooner than 20 days after the notice of proposed rulemaking is published and at least 10 days before the end of the comment period.[16] Notice of the public meeting must appear in the same publication as the proposed rule. The agency must also include any information it received during the comment period and any information that it considered.

To avoid stale rulemaking proposals, the Model Act includes a provision that if the agency does not adopt a final rule within two years of the publication of the proposed rule, it must terminate the rulemaking.[17] It may, however, for good cause, extend the

---

[13] MSAPA § 304(a).

[14] MSAPA § 304(b).

[15] MSAPA § 305(c).

[16] MSAPA § 306(c).

[17] MSAPA § 307(b).

time for issuing the rule for two additional years if it publishes a statement of good cause and reopens the comment period.[18]

iv. Final Rule Issuance

The Model Act requires the agency to publish the final rule in the state's official publication for rules. The final rule notice must contain the text of the final rule and a record containing the following key information about the rule: (i) date of adoption and effective date of rule; (ii) citation to the specific statutory authorization for the rule; (iii) any finding required by law before adoption or effectiveness of the rule; and (iv) a concise explanation of the rule.[19]

The agency must also include in the explanation of the rule a statement that contains an explanation of why the agency is adopting the rule and a summary of the regulatory analysis prepared in conjunction with the proposed rule. In addition, it must explain the reasons for any changes between the proposed and final rule.[20] The requirement that a final rule must be a "logical outgrowth" of the proposed rule is codified in the Model Act.[21] This is a test developed in the case law at both the federal and state level. If an agency decides to change its stance significantly after hearing comments on a proposed rule such that the new action is not fairly seen as a logical outgrowth of the original proposal, it may do so, but it will have to re-propose the rule and seek additional comment. The goal of the rulemaking notice is to ensure potentially interested parties the opportunity to provide meaningful comment. If the agency fundamentally changes the rule, then interested parties would not have fair notice. For this reason, the agency must re-propose the rule and alternatives under consideration. Courts will look to determine whether changes in the final rule were reasonably foreseeable actions based on the rule proposal.

When drafting a notice of a proposed rulemaking, the rule drafter should make clear potential alternatives being considered and ensure that the scope of the notice covers the range of options under consideration. A rule drafter may even consider proposing alternative language to make clear various options under consideration. As noted above, the advanced notice of a proposed rulemaking is an informal mechanism to solicit early comments on a range of options and avoid re-proposal later.

v. Petition for Rulemaking

The Model Act in section 318 provides that a party may petition an agency to commence a rulemaking procedure. An agency can prescribe the requirements for its consideration of the petition and action on the petition. The agency must act on the petition within a specified period of time. A denial of a petition for rulemaking is considered a final agency action and is typically subject to judicial review. If the desired action is discretionary, then courts will give broad deference to an agency in

---

[18] *Id.*

[19] MSAPA § 312.

[20] MSAPA § 313.

[21] *See* MSAPA § 308.

denying a petition. If, however, an agency action is mandated by statute, then the agency may be compelled to act to comply with the statutory requirement.

e.   Executive Review of Agency Rulemaking

While most agencies at the state level are a part of the executive branch over which a governor has control, the agencies often operate relatively independently of the governor's office if a formal review process was not established. In addition, at the state level, while states have counterparts to federal agencies, there are many commissions or boards which oversee the work of an agency, or are indeed the rulemaking entity for those agencies. While a governor may appoint members of those boards, they are typically for set terms and do not automatically change with each change of governor. In an era where there is a substantial public sentiment for a smaller government and less burdensome regulations, some executives at the state level have stepped up their oversight of state rulemakings by executive branch agencies.

One notable example of such an effort was in Wisconsin in 2011. The state enacted legislation requiring approval by the governor's office before an agency can proceed with rulemaking.[22] Under the Act, and subsequent Executive Order 50, an agency must submit an initial "Statement of Scope" statement to the governor's office before doing any other work on the rulemaking. The governor's office must review and approve the statement of scope before the statement by the legislative reference bureau can publish and the rulemaking proceed.[23] The statement of scope must include detailed information including: the legislative authority for the rule; existing policies relevant to the rule and new policies to be included in the rule; a description of all entities that may be impacted by the rule; the estimated impact of the rule; and staff time needed to undertake the rulemaking.[24] In addition to requiring formal approval by the governor, the legislation and executive order require a comprehensive economic impact analysis to be performed on any proposed rule that is to become a permanent rule.[25] The governor has set forth very detailed requirements for an agency to solicit input of affected parties in conducting the economic impact analysis.[26] While this process may be one of the more rigorous procedures established for gubernatorial oversight of agency rulemakings, other states often will have some kind of informal review process to ensure agency rules are not inconsistent with the general policy positions of the governor.

---

[22] Wis. Stat. §§ 227.135(2); 227.24(1)(e)1d.; Executive Order 50, Relating to Guidelines for the Promulgation of Administrative Rules, § II.1.

[23] *See* Executive Order 50, at § II.

[24] *Id.*

[25] Wis. Stat. § 227.137.

[26] Executive Order 50, § IV.

f. Legislative Oversight of Agency Rulemaking

In many states, the legislature retains some kind of oversight of agency rulemaking actions. The review process is typically a more vigorous and routine part of the rulemaking process than Congressional review of federal agency rulemakings. Legislative oversight at the state level takes on many forms. According to the National Conference of State Legislatures, 41 states have some legislative oversight of agency rules.[27] In some cases, legislative review is the end of the rulemaking process and is limited in scope. In other states, a legislative committee will review and may hold public hearings on proposed rules before they become final. In states in which the legislature has veto power over agency rules, 13 states require enactment of a statute and 15 states require passage of a resolution before a rule becomes final. Lastly, in a few states, the legislature must ratify all rules adopted by an agency before they become effective.

For example, in Ohio, a Joint Committee on Agency Rule Review consisting of five members of the house and five members of the senate are responsible for reviewing proposed and adopted rules.[28] In Ohio, the joint committee does not have the authority to reject a proposed rule. That power is vested with the General Assembly but the committee will make recommendations to the General Assembly.[29] The General Assembly can invalidate a rule for a number of different reasons under Ohio law including that the rule: exceeds the agency's authority; conflicts with legislative intent; or fails to demonstrate that the rule's intent justifies the adverse impact on business.[30] If a rule is invalidated by the General Assembly, an agency may not adopt a similar rule for the duration of that legislative session.[31]

In Colorado, all executive branch agency rules are subject to expiration on May 15 of the year following the rule's issuance unless the general assembly passes a bill to postpone expiration.[32] Thus, rather than acting in a veto capacity, the legislature allows rules it does not like to expire and lets the remaining rules continue by passing a bill to extend those rules.[33]

Below is a diagram of the Colorado rulemaking process.

---

[27] National Conference of State Legislatures, *Separation of Powers — Legislative Oversight*, available at www.ncsl.org/.

[28] Ohio Legislative Service Commission, *A Guidebook for Ohio Legislators*, at 75 (2011).

[29] *Id.*

[30] *Id.* at 74-75.

[31] *Id.* at 75.

[32] Office of Legislative Services, Colorado General Assembly, *Frequently Asked Questions*, August, 2, 2011.

[33] *Id.*

PERMANENT RULEMAKING PROCESS

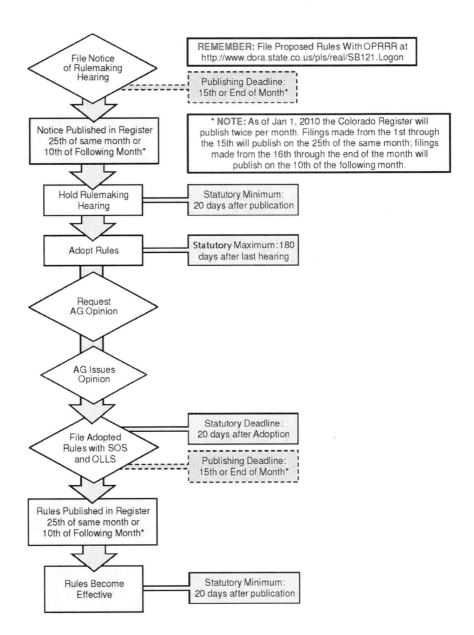

File Notice of Rulemaking Hearing

REMEMBER: File Proposed Rules With OPRRR at http://www.dora.state.co.us/pls/real/SB121.Logon

Publishing Deadline: 15th or End of Month*

Notice Published in Register 25th of same month or 10th of Following Month*

* NOTE: As of Jan 1, 2010 the Colorado Register will publish twice per month. Filings made from the 1st through the 15th will publish on the 25th of the same month; filings made from the 16th through the end of the month will publish on the 10th of the following month.

Hold Rulemaking Hearing

Statutory Minimum: 20 days after publication

Adopt Rules

Statutory Maximum: 180 days after last hearing

Request AG Opinion

AG Issues Opinion

File Adopted Rules with SOS and OLLS

Statutory Deadline: 20 days after Adoption

Publishing Deadline: 15th or End of Month*

Rules Published in Register 25th of same month or 10th of Following Month*

Rules Become Effective

Statutory Minimum: 20 days after publication

Colorado Secretary of State • Administrative Rules Program • 1700 Broadway, Suite 300 • Denver CO 80290 • 303-894-2200 • www.sos.state.co.us

g. Judicial Review of Agency Rulemaking

In administrative law, there is a general presumption in favor of judicial review of a final agency action, and the Model Act so provides.[34] It defines *"final agency action"* as an *"act of an agency which imposes an obligation, grants or denies a right, confers a benefit . . . ."*[35] A failure to act is not considered a final action. However, a court may compel an agency to take an action that is unlawfully withheld or unreasonably delayed.[36] A person may also seek judicial review of a non-final action if postponement of judicial review would result in an inadequate remedy or irreparable harm that outweighs the public benefit derived from postponing review.[37]

A stay of the effectiveness of the rule is not automatic upon filing judicial review, but a party may seek a stay.[38] A court can issue a stay on the same grounds as under the rules of civil procedure.

In seeking judicial review, the Model Act follows the general principle found in many state acts that a party must exhaust all required administrative remedies before seeking judicial review. The Act does not require a petition for reconsideration as a prerequisite for judicial review. If, however, a party files a petition for reconsideration, then the time for filing for judicial review of the agency action is tolled and a person may not seek review while the petition for reconsideration is pending.[39] The Model Act does not require a party to file an administrative petition for reconsideration.

Interestingly, the Model Act does not require a party to have participated in a rulemaking proceeding to challenge a rule.[40] For this reason, the Act appears to allow a person to challenge an agency rule, without having to raise an objection during the rulemaking process. Many state and federal provisions state otherwise. The concept of standing is codified in the Model Act. It provides standing for a person aggrieved or adversely affected by the agency action or to whom standing is given by another state law.[41]

3. Local Government Rulemaking

Local governments use a wide variety of procedures in enacting local rules. As is noted in Chapter 6[C], there are few procedural requirements for local legislation. The process for the adoption of a rule by a local government agency is even more chaotic. Few local jurisdictions have formal publications such as a local version of a federal register to publicize proposed rulemakings or local legislation, so it is often

---

[34] MSAPA § 501.

[35] *Id.* This definition, not coincidentally, is the same as the classic definition of a law, as discussed in Chapter 9.

[36] MSAPA § 501(a) and (d).

[37] MSAPA § 501(c).

[38] MSAPA § 504.

[39] MSAPA §§ 503(d) and 506.

[40] MSAPA § 506(c).

[41] MSAPA § 505.

difficult to keep abreast of local government rulemaking actions.

Many local citizens complain that it is difficult to know about local government legislative activity and thus difficult to participate in those activities. The problem is even worse for local agency rules, because there is little or no notice of the rulemaking process or of a rule when it is finally adopted. The problem is exacerbated by the fact that there are so many local government units, and each one has multiple agencies that adopt rules. These include schools, health departments and hospitals, zoning agencies, building departments, recreational facilities, tax assessors, road and transportation entities, business licensing, and so on infinitum. They affect more people in more ways than federal and state rules combined, yet there are no standards for how the rules are developed, adopted, publicized, or enforced.

The Model State Administrative Procedure Act can provide a good template for local governments in evaluating how to provide for meaningful opportunity for public involvement in adopting local ordinances or rules. While it may be difficult for local communities to have resources to provide for formal response to comments, the Model Act can be a useful guide on public notice provisions, dissemination of information, and ensuring that in some way public comment is considered and addressed by the local rulemaking entity. Local governments should also make provision for judicial review of local rules.

B.   COURT RULES

Chapter 3[B] describes the rulemaking power of the federal courts as limited to practice and procedure rules under a Congressional grant of authority, the Rules Enabling Act. The situation in state courts is far different, both as to the sources of authority and the subject matters covered.

1.   Sources of Authority and Subjects Covered

A state court, and in particular a state supreme court, has potentially three sources of rulemaking authority — constitutional, inherent, and statutory. There has been a trend over the past several decades to grant explicit rulemaking authority to state supreme courts in state constitutions, especially in the fields of bar admission and lawyer discipline, practice and procedure, court administration, and judicial conduct and discipline.

Beginning in colonial times, state supreme courts and local courts adopted their own procedural rules and decided whom to admit to practice before them, acting under their own inherent authority to control the proceedings before them. As time progressed, legislatures first regulated both the legal profession and court procedure. Later, they gave state supreme courts statewide authority over both subjects, but usually reserving legislative authority to amend a rule the supreme court adopted.[42]

---

[42] *See generally* Wolf, *Inherent Rulemaking Authority of an Independent Judiciary*, 56 Miami L. Rev. 507 (2002); R. Martineau, Regulation of the Legal Profession: Relationship between Judicial and Legislative Power (1987) (published as a report of the National Center for State Courts).

State supreme court power over statewide court administration and judicial conduct, especially the power to discipline or remove a judge, came only from constitutional amendments adopted in the past half century. Previously there was only limited statewide court administration, usually starting with a statutorily authorized state court administrator who had little direct authority. The only power over judicial discipline was impeachment, which was seldom utilized, or the elective process under which judges are elected for a specified term.

Probably the most powerful influence on the expansion of state supreme court authority over the administration of justice in a state has been the American Bar Association. The ABA began over a century ago urging the adoption of statewide educational standards for those seeking admission to the bar and for discipline of lawyers. As noted above, state legislatures first exercised this control, but over time, statutes or constitutional amendments transferred control to the state supreme court. The ABA has also led the drive for statewide court administration, standards of judicial conduct, and a system of judicial discipline administered under the supervision of the state supreme court.[43]

Thanks to these efforts by the ABA, most state supreme courts now have express constitutional authority over rules of procedure, bar admissions and lawyer conduct and discipline, judicial conduct and discipline, and court administration. Only in the area of procedure and bar regulation do legislatures retain any authority, and what little they have they seldom exercise. When there is a conflict, the general rule is that the body that speaks last prevails, but that is only until the other body takes further action. It sounds messy, but a legislature seldom interferes with rules or actions of a supreme court. If an effort is made by a legislature, it is usually at the urging of an individual legislator who has been personally involved in a matter and who is unhappy with the action taken by the supreme court. The effort is seldom successful.

Courts make rules governing four principal areas — procedure, court administration, the legal profession, and judges. The rules that have the broadest effect are procedural. That is because they affect both lawyers and litigants at all court levels, and at each step of the legal process from the filing and serving of a complaint to the enforcement of a judgment after review in the state supreme court. The basic classifications are trial and appellate, but often expand to civil and criminal, small claims, domestic relations and family, juvenile, probate, and traffic, intermediate appellate, and supreme court. There are also statewide rules and those for only a particular judicial district.

2. Rulemaking Process

Initially, there was no statewide control over the legal profession or court procedure. Each court, local or state, adopted its own procedural rules, usually copied from some other jurisdiction. Each court admitted lawyers to practice before it, either on evidence that the lawyer had been admitted to practice before another court, even

---

[43] The ABA began a project in the mid-1970s to develop Standards for the Administration of Justice. For a review of this effort, see G. Griller, E. Stott § J. Fallahay, The Improvement of the Administration of Justice (7th ed., 2002), published by the ABA.

in another state, or on the motion of an already admitted lawyer that a person seeking admission for the first time had studied with the lawyer and had gained sufficient knowledge to qualify the applicant to practice law. Legal education in an academic setting was rare, and lasted a year at most.

As states grew in population and economic activity, there was a recognition that a statewide system was needed for both regulation of the legal profession and procedural rules. At first it was done by the legislature. Only in the early twentieth century did state supreme courts begin to play a role in the regulation of both fields. When courts started exercising rulemaking power, they usually acted, as is typical of all governmental institutions, by appointing a committee. The committee would meet privately, draft rules, and present them to the court. The court would consider them privately and then issue an order adopting them. Public participation in the process was minimal. This was especially true for rules of procedure, the area that had broadest effect on both lawyers and the public in general.

Today there are two principal vehicles for the development of supreme court rules. One, the most common, is for a supreme court to appoint an advisory committee to draft and submit proposals to the court. In other states, this role is assigned by statute to an independent body, usually called a judicial council.[44]

As the power of the courts, and particularly of state supreme courts, has expanded to be the dominant, if not exclusive, regulator in the areas of lawyers, judges, court procedure, and court administration, the demand for opening up the process for developing the rules governing these subjects has similarly expanded. The process now usually includes the holding of hearings, publication of draft rules, solicitation of comments, and revisions of the proposed rules on the basis of those comments. Final action by the supreme court is usually only a formality.

The drafting quality of the rules adopted by a supreme court reflects, unfortunately, the drafting abilities of most lawyers, that is anywhere between poor and awful. This is to be expected because those who draft rules for supreme court advisory committees are usually selected for their substantive expertise, not their drafting abilities. Unlike recent developments in the federal system, state supreme courts have shown little recognition of the importance of rules that are not only substantively correct but well drafted. The situation in states with judicial councils is usually better because they have permanent staff who develop drafting expertise.

---

[44] McKay, *Use of Judicial Councils and Conferences, in* American Bar Assoc., The Improvement of the Administration of Justice 113-126 (6th ed. 1981).

Chapter 5

STATUTES AND RULES IN THE COURTS

A. THE MEANING OF STATUTORY INTERPRETATION OR CONSTRUCTION

After a legislative body enacts a statute or an administrative agency adopts a rule, the first persons to interpret the statute or rule are those who have the task of implementing it, such as an administrative agency, government official, or a private party who may be affected by its terms. If one or more words in the statute or rule becomes the basis of a dispute between parties, either governmental or private, and one of them asks a court to resolve the dispute, the court will then interpret the words and apply that interpretation to resolve the dispute. The act of the court interpreting the statutory or rule language is what is known as statutory interpretation or construction. The two words are used interchangeably, but those who use the terms, especially judges and legal scholars, mean only judicial action and not interpretation or construction by anyone else.

It could be argued that interpretation and construction are two separate processes. Under this approach, interpretation involves only what a word in the statute or rule means in the definitional sense, while construction involves applying that meaning to resolve a dispute. That is not the case. The two terms have become synonyms. For some reason, judges use the term statutory construction and scholars statutory interpretation. In this book, we will use statutory interpretation. (Interestingly, the best known book on statutory interpretation, Sutherland on Statutes and Statutory Construction, uses the term statutory interpretation in its text.)

B. THE IMPORTANCE OF STATUTORY AND RULE INTERPRETATION TO THE DRAFTER

Although the drafter of a statute or rule is not directly concerned with litigation over the meaning of the words the drafter has chosen to include in a statute or rule, the drafter should be aware of what evidence courts will consider and the terminology they use in interpreting a statute. With this awareness, the drafter can attempt to avoid word choices that would allow a court to construe a statute in a way clearly not intended by the statute or rule's drafter, proponent, or sponsor. The drafter may not always be successful in this endeavor, but the drafter's goal should be to keep these occasions to a minimum.

C. STATUTORY RULES OF INTERPRETATION

The most important rules of statutory and rule interpretation of which the drafter should be aware are those enacted by the legislative body of the relevant jurisdiction. A court will look first at these rules when the statute or rule becomes the subject of litigation. Notwithstanding the primacy of these rules, in fact they are of relatively little importance because generally they deal with only minor issues such as whether the singular includes plural and the masculine includes the feminine. Each state has enacted some rules of interpretation law so the drafter of a state statute or rule must be familiar with the applicable state provisions.

The National Conference of Commissioners on Uniform State Laws in 1995 adopted a Uniform Statute and Rule Construction Act in an effort to promote statutory interpretation acts. This effort has not been met with success, New Mexico being the only state enacting it.[1]

Another proposal at the federal level was for the adoption of rules of statutory interpretation following the model of other federal rules of procedure.[2] Yet another proposal was for the American Law Institute to prepare a Restatement of Statutory Interpretation.[3] These latter two proposals did not get even as far as the Uniform Laws effort.

There are three reasons why the efforts to codify rules of construction in a statute, court rule, or restatement have been a failure. The first is that these rules are primarily concerned with the simpler aspects of statutory interpretation. The second reason is because while they attempted to go somewhat beyond the very limited state interpretation acts already on the books, they did not go far enough to be of help to the courts in difficult cases.[4] By and large, they do not get into the far more difficult areas of the canons of construction or interpretation that go to how the courts weigh and balance the various considerations that are the subject of the canons. More importantly, however, is that all of these proposals fail to realize that the canons are, in difficult cases, merely the means by which judges explain and justify their application of a statute to the facts of the case before them. They are not the bases that led them to that result and thus are not decisive in the resolution of the case.[5]

---

[1] Uniform Law Commission, Legislative Fact Sheet-Statute and Rule Construction Act (2012). The New Mexico adoption is codified in N.M. Stat. Ann. §§ 12-2A-1 et seq.

[2] Rosenkranz, *Federal Rules of Statutory Interpretation*, 115 Harv. L. Rev. 2085 (2002).

[3] O'Connor, *Restatement (First) of Statutory Interpretation*, 7 N.Y.U. J. Legis. & Pub. Pol'y 333 (2003-04).

[4] Comment, *The Uniform Statute and Rule Construction Act: Help, Hindrance, or Irrelevancy?*, 44 Kan. L. Rev. 423, 456-58 (1996).

[5] Martineau, *Craft and Technique, Not Canons and Grand Theories: A Neo-Realist View of Statutory Construction*, 62 Geo. Wash. L. Rev. 1 (1993); Llewellyn, *Remarks on the Theory of Appellate Decision and the Rules of Canons About How Statutes Are to Be Construed*, 3 Vand. L. Rev. 395 (1950); Comment, *The Uniform Statute and Rule Construction Act, supra* note 4.

Another type of legislative effort to control courts in interpreting a statute or rule is "plain meaning" statutes. These statutes have been adopted in nine states.[6] These statutes may, such as Connecticut's, simply provide that if the language of the statute is plain and unambiguous, a court may not consider extra-textual evidence of the statute's meaning. Others are more like North Dakota and Louisiana which provide that when *"the wording of a statute is clear and free from all ambiguity, the letter of it may not be disregarded under the pretext of pursuing its spirit."*[7]

These "plain meaning" statutes usually result from a judicial decision interpreting a statute with which the current members of the legislature disagree. It can be seen from the statutes' language, however, that they are not likely to have much effect. By their terms, they apply only when the language of the statute under consideration is clear and unambiguous. Few courts are likely to resort to other considerations in such cases. More importantly, if a court really wants to find lack of clarity or ambiguity in a statute, it can easily do so. One judge, in commenting on the Connecticut statute, put it as well as it could be stated:

> *The legislative renewal of the plain meaning rule, in any form, reveals an inter-branch tension that may have some effect on the ongoing debate about the role of judges in a statutory era. However, in the process of adjudication, once a determination has been made that a statute is either unclear or ambiguous, or that its application would reap an unworkable result, a court will likely carry out its interpretive function guided by its own best adjudicative judgment, resorting or not to extrinsic sources, unaffected by the . . . plain meaning rule.*[8]

D.   THE LITERATURE ON STATUTORY INTERPRETATION[9]

In the world of modern legal literature, few subjects have attracted more attention than statutory interpretation. In part that is because we are, as the famous expression goes, in the "Age of Statutes"[10] (not to mention rules). In addition, we are more than ever a litigious society. The combination necessarily results in courts having to decide an ever increasing number of cases in which the interpretation of a statute or rule determines the result.

As might be expected, this world is largely populated by law professors along with a few judges (most of whom were previously law professors). If there is a starting point for this academic focus, it is the 1930 article *Statutory Interpretation* by Professor Max Radin published in the Harvard Law Review.[11] In this article, Professor Radin

---

[6] Bishop, *The Death and Reincarnation of Plain Meaning in Connecticut: A Case Study*, 41 Conn. L. Rev. 825, 855 (2009).

[7] *Id.* at 856.

[8] *Id.* at 860.

[9] For a fuller treatment of the the development of the approaches to statutory interpretation over the years, see Martineau, *supra* note 5, at 1-23.

[10] G. Calabresi, A Common Law for the Age of Statutes (1982).

[11] Radin, *Statutory Interpretation*, 43 Harv. L. Rev. 863 (1930).

challenged the almost universally held view (then and now) that the function of a court in interpreting a statute is to discover and carry out the intent of the legislature. His opinion was that you should not try to discover this intent because it is impossible to do so. His argued that when several hundred legislators vote for a bill, no one knows what each one is thinking, but it is certain that they are not all thinking the same thing about each word in a bill that may be hundreds of pages long. Under such circumstances, he concluded that there can be no such thing as a single, discoverable legislative intent.[12]

Radin went on to argue that plain meaning, intent, and purpose gave no certain answer to the question of how a statute is to be applied in a particular case to a particular set of facts. More realistically, the judge will decide the issue on the basis of the whole range of influences that guide a judge to make a choice, including precedent and the background of the judge. According to Radin, the best we can hope for is that *"the sound sense of many judges will frequently penetrate this smoke screen and reach results that seem satisfactory, but it is often done half-consciously and almost surreptitiously."*[13]

Unfortunately, this effort at legal realism did not gain much traction. Rather, beginning in 1958, Harvard law professors Hart and Sachs developed the approach of looking to the overall purpose of a statute to guide its interpretation.[14] They and others taught this approach to several generations of Harvard law students, and it gained wide acceptance in legal education.

The next major development was the publication of Professors Eskridge and Frickey's book *Legislation* in 1988. This book and their other writings made legislation, and in particular statutory interpretation, one of the hot topics of legal education and legal literature. They divided theories of statutory interpretation between textualist and contextual. This division meant nothing more than whether a judge in applying a statute in a case is limited to the words of the statute or can go outside of it and look at other things such as purpose.

In more recent writings, they have classified previous approaches to statutory interpretation as focusing on legislative intent, legislative purpose, or simply textual. After finding fault with all three, they came up with their own, which they termed *"practical reasoning."*[15] This they define to mean that a court relies on a broad range of evidence to ascertain how to apply a statute to a particular set of facts. Usually all factors point to the same result. In hard cases, however, the evidence is conflicting. Then *"the court critically analyzes each textual or historical or evaluative argument, both as to its own cogency and as to its cogency in light of other evidence."*[16]

---

[12] *Id.* at 870-71.

[13] *Id.* at 882.

[14] H. Hart, Jr. & A. Sacks, The Legal Process: Basic Problems in the Making and Application of Law (tent. ed., 1958).

[15] Eskridge & Frickey, *Statutory Interpretation as Practical Reasoning*, 42 Stan. L. Rev. 321 (1990).

[16] *Id.* at 323.

Other major contributors to the literature have been Karl Llewellyn, Justice Scalia, Judge Posner as well as Professors Cass Sunstein and Reed Dickerson and a host of others. The outpouring has been so great that Judge Posner has described it as *"cacophonous."*[17]

For the authors, the approach that makes the most sense is the one developed by Karl Llewellyn in a 1950 law review article and expanded upon by Professor Martineau in a 1993 article.[18] In their view, judges (at least judges who did not come to the bench from academia) do not apply a statute or rule to the facts of a case by first adopting some theory of statutory interpretation or canon of construction. Rather they decide first on what is a fair and reasonable result in the case taking into consideration both the facts of the case and the words of the statute. This is generally done in the decision conference on the case either after oral argument or, if none, on the briefs. It then becomes the task of the judge assigned to write the opinion in the case to come up with justifications for the decision. These justifications can be based solely on the text of the statute or rule or, if the text does not produce an easy result, on other factors both internal to the statute or rule or external to it. These internal and external factors are discussed in the following sections.

E. CANONS OF CONSTRUCTION LIMITED TO STATUTORY OR RULE TEXT

When a judge writes an opinion explaining the court's application of a statute or rule to the facts of the case and there is any disagreement as to the meaning of one or more words in the statute or rule, usually the first resort is to the canons of construction. These canons are primarily conventions on the use of language that most people follow in every day life, whether speaking or writing. They are at best presumptions that can be followed or ignored at will. The biggest mistake judges make in the use of canons is to treat them as inflexible rules that must be followed even if they produce an unfair or absurd result. The canons have long been criticized, the most famous being Karl Llewellyn's showing that for most canons there are opposing ones that lead to an opposite result.[19]

Not withstanding these criticisms, judges continue to use the canons in opinions to justify the application of a statute or rule in particular cases. For this reason, the statutory or rule drafter must be familiar with the canons and, when possible, comply with them to avoid unnecessary complications in the interpretation of a statute or rule.

There are many canons of construction and many statements of them. Perhaps the most famous of the statements are those of Karl Llewellyn in his famous criticism of them. They include:

    1. If language is plain and unambiguous it must be given effect.

---

[17] Posner, *Legislation and Its Interpretation: A Primer*, 68 Neb. L. Rev. 431, 434 (1989).

[18] Martineau, *supra* note 5; Llewellyn, *supra* note 5.

[19] Llewellyn, *supra* note 5.

2. Words are to be taken in their ordinary meaning unless they are technical terms or words of art.

3. Every word and clause must be given effect.

4. The same language used repeatedly in the same connection is presumed to bear the same meaning throughout the statute.

5. Words are to be interpreted according to the proper grammatical effect of their arrangement within the statute.

6. Expression of one thing excludes another.

7. General terms are to receive a general construction.

8. [W]here general words follow an enumeration, they are to be held as applying only to persons and things of the same general kind or class specifically mentioned (ejusdem generis).

9. Qualifying or limiting words or clauses are to be referred to the next preceding antecedent.

10. Punctuation will govern when a statute is open to two constructions.

11. There is a distinction between words of permission and mandatory words.

12. Titles do not control meaning; preambles do not expand scope; section headings do not change language.

13. A statute cannot go beyond its text.[20]

These statements of the canons by Llewellyn are not remarkable. What is remarkable is that for each canon he found another canon, with citation, that stated exactly the opposite. It was because he determined that for each canon there was a canon stating exactly the opposite that he developed his thesis that a particular canon is chosen by a court, not as a basis for leading it to a conclusion as to how to apply the statute in the case before it, but only as a justification for the conclusion based on other considerations.

While Llewellyn's analysis has been the subject of various criticism, his statements of the canons are presented here to show the how the canons are commonly phrased. The drafter of a statute or rule can select the words for inclusion in the statute or rule in light of them. They are essentially just principles of good writing that should guide the drafter but with the knowledge that a court can ignore them at will.

---

[20] *Id., reprinted in* K. Llewellyn, The Common Law Tradition: Deciding Appeals 521-535 (1960). While canons listed are quotations, their numbering has been changed.

F. CANONS OF CONSTRUCTION CONCERNING SOURCES OUTSIDE THE TEXT

There is substantial debate over the extent to which a court may look outside the text of a statue or rule to ascertain its meaning, particularly as to its legislative history. Notwithstanding that debate, it is a fact of statutory and rule interpretation that courts often do so.

A court generally starts its interpretative analysis with a recital of the *"plain meaning rule."* This rule holds that a court may not look at external sources when *"the language is plain and admits of no more than one meaning, the duty of interpretation does not arise, and the rules which are said to aid doubtful meanings need no discussion."*[21] The reality, of course, is that plain meaning often depends on the eye of the beholder. When one judge may see only one meaning, another may see two or more possible meanings. Under the Llewellyn analysis, that resort is not so much an effort to discover the obscure meaning of a word, but to support the result the court believes is just in the case.

The courts have developed canons for using outside sources just as they have done with those limited to the text of the statute. Again, using the formulations of Llewellyn, they include:

1. Statutes in derogation of the common law will not be extended by construction.

2. Where a foreign statute which has received construction has been adopted, previous construction is adopted too.

3. Where various states have already adopted the statute, the parent state is followed.

4. Statutes in pari materia *must be construed together.*

5. Words and phrases which have received judicial construction are to be understood according to that construction.

6. After enactment, judicial interpretation of particular terms and phrases controls [not executive interpretation].

7. A statutory provision requiring liberal construction does not mean disregard of unequivocal requirements of the statute.[22]

As with internal canons, Llewellyn set forth an opposing canon for each of his external canons.

---

[21] *Caminetti v. United States*, 242 U.S. 470, 485 (1917).

[22] Llewellyn, note 19 *supra*. Again, these canons are quotations but the numbering has been changed.

G. LEGISLATIVE HISTORY

A special type of outside source is the legislative history of a statute or rule. If a court decides to look at the legislative history of a statute or rule, it has a host of sources to which it can refer. They include: floor debates, reports of committees that either produced the statute or rule or reviewed the statute or rule, reports of executive agencies that drafted or reviewed the rule, opposing or supporting testimony, analyses by reviewing bodies such as legislative agencies assigned that task, amendments adopted or rejected at any stage of the drafting, enactment, or adoption process. In other words, the sources include any official discussion that preceded the enactment or adoption.

Although there are some critics, Justice Scalia being the most outspoken and prolific,[23] most courts do look at legislative history materials to justify their application of the text in the case.

Interestingly, the one source that may be the most relevant to what a word in a statute or rule means is the testimony of the person who actually did the drafting and chose the word being interpreted. The almost universal rule is that this testimony is not admissible in court and is not considered.

The canon stated above relating to executive interpretation, no. 6, has been severely modified by the Supreme Court. In the *Chevron* case,[24] the Court adopted the rule that the interpretation of a statute by the agency given responsibility for administering it was to be followed unless it was unreasonable or contrary to a specific intent of Congress. Some commentators thought the rule went too far, and in some subsequent cases, the Court appeared to give less deference to the administrative interpretation than the language of *Chevron* seems to call for, although it has not expressly overturned the case. (See Chapter 3 above for additional discussion of *Chevron*).

For the prudent statute or rule drafter, the key lesson to learn from the foregoing discussion is that it is impossible to predict how a court will construe and apply a statute or rule in any given case. There are simply too many variables in terms of overriding judicial philosophy of the judges, the equities of the case, the quality of counsel, the financial implications of the decision, or any of the other factors that make litigation so unpredictable. All the drafter can do is to be as careful and precise as possible and hope (and perhaps pray) that the drafter has chosen the words in a statute or rule with such care that a court interpreting it has no choice but to interpret and apply it as the drafter, proponent, and sponsor intended.

---

[23] *See, e.g.*, A. Scalia, A Matter of Interpretation: Federal Courts and the Law (1997).

[24] *Chevron U.S.A., Inc. v. Natural Resources Def. Council, Inc.*, 467 U.S. 837 (1984).

PART III

CONSTITUTIONAL AND LEGISLATIVE RULES
GOVERNING STRUCTURE OF A BILL

Chapter 6

MANDATORY FORM AND LANGUAGE

The first step for the drafter in drafting a bill (or other type of legislation) is to become familiar with the requirements as to form and language of the bill. These requirements can be constitutional, statutory, rule based, or simply customary. To avoid complications in the enactment process, or more importantly in any subsequent court proceeding involving the statute, the drafter must ensure that the bill is correct both as to form and language.

A. FEDERAL

The best summary of the forms of various types of federal legislative actions is in "How Our Laws Are Made" published by the U.S. Government Printing Office. Chapter IV reads as follows:

FORMS OF CONGRESSIONAL ACTION

The work of Congress is initiated by the introduction of a proposal in one of four forms: the bill, the joint resolution, the concurrent resolution, and the simple resolution. The most customary form used in both Houses is the bill. During the 109th Congress (2005-2006), 10,558 bills and 143 joint resolutions were introduced in both Houses. Of the total number introduced, 6,436 bills and 102 joint resolutions originated in the House of Representatives.

For the purpose of simplicity, this discussion will be confined generally to the procedure on a measure of the House of Representatives, with brief comment on each of the forms.

BILLS

A bill is the form used for most legislation, whether permanent or temporary, general or special, public or private.

The form of a House bill is as follows:

A BILL

For the establishment, etc. (as the title may be).
Be it enacted by the Senate and House of Representatives of the United States of America in Congress assembled, That, etc.

The enacting clause was prescribed by law in 1871 and is identical in all bills, whether they originate in the House of Representatives or in the Senate.

By tradition, general appropriation bills also originate in the House of Representatives.

Bills may originate in either the House of Representatives or the Senate with one notable exception. Article I, Section 7, of the Constitution provides that all bills for raising revenue shall originate in the House of Representatives but that the Senate may propose, or concur with, amendments.

There are two types of bills — public and private. A public bill is one that affects the public generally. A bill that affects a specified individual or private entity rather than the population at large is called a private bill. A typical private bill is used for relief in matters such as immigration and naturalization and claims against the United States.

A bill originating in the House of Representatives is designated by "H.R." followed by a number that it retains throughout all its parliamentary stages. The letters signify "House of Representatives" and not, as is sometimes incorrectly assumed, "House resolution." A Senate bill is designated by "S." followed by its number. The term "companion bill" is used to describe a bill introduced in one House of Congress that is similar or identical to a bill introduced in the other House of Congress.

A bill that has been agreed to in identical form by both bodies becomes the law of the land only after —

1. *Presidential approval; or*

2. *failure by the President to return it with objections to the House in which it originated within 10 days (Sundays excepted) while Congress is in session; or*

3. *the overriding of a presidential veto by a two-thirds vote in each House.*

Such a bill does not become law without the President's signature if Congress by their final adjournment prevent its return with objections. This is known as a "pocket veto." For a discussion of presidential action on legislation, see Part XVIII.

JOINT RESOLUTIONS

Joint resolutions may originate either in the House of Representatives or in the Senate — not, as is sometimes incorrectly assumed, jointly in both Houses. There is little practical difference between a bill and a joint resolution and the two forms are sometimes used interchangeably. One difference in form is that a joint resolution may include a preamble preceding the resolving clause. Statutes that have been initiated as bills may be amended by a joint resolution and vice versa. Both are subject to the same procedure except for a joint resolution proposing an amendment to the Constitution. When a joint resolution amending the Constitution is approved by two-thirds of both Houses, it is not presented to the President for approval. Rather, such a joint resolution is sent directly to the Archivist of the United

States for submission to the several states where ratification by the legislatures of three-fourths of the states within the period of time prescribe in the joint resolution is necessary for the amendment to become part of the Constitution.

JOINT RESOLUTION

Authorizing, etc. [as the title may be]. Resolved by the Senate and the House of Representatives of the United States of America in Congress assembled, That, etc.

The resolving clause is identical in both House and Senate joint resolutions as has been prescribed by statute since 1871. It is frequently preceded by a preamble consisting of one or more "where-as" clauses indicating the necessity for or the desirability of the joint resolution.

A joint resolution originating in the House of Representatives is designated "H.J. Res." followed by its individual number which it retains throughout all its parliamentary stages. One originating in the Senate is designated "S.J. Res." followed by its number.

Joint resolutions, with the exception of proposed amendments to the Constitution, become law in the same manner as bills.

CONCURRENT RESOLUTIONS

A matter affecting the operations of both Houses is usually initiated by a concurrent resolution. In modern practice, and as determined by the Supreme Court in INS v. Chadha, 463 U.S. 919 (1983), concurrent and simple resolutions normally are not legislative in character since not "presented" to the President for approval, but are used merely for expressing facts, principles, opinions, and purposes of the two Houses. A concurrent resolution is not equivalent to a bill and its use is narrowly limited within these bounds. The term "concurrent", like "joint", does not signify simultaneous introduction and consideration in both Houses.

A concurrent resolution originating in the House of Representatives is designated "H. Con. Res." followed by its individual number, while a Senate concurrent resolution is designated "S. Con. Res." together with its number. On approval by both Houses, they are signed by the Clerk of the House of the Secretary of the Senate and transmitted to the Archivist of the United States for publication in a special part of the Statutes at Large volume covering that session of Congress.

SIMPLE RESOLUTIONS

A matter concerning the rules, the operation, or the opinion of either House alone is initiated by a simple resolution. A resolution affecting the House of Representatives is designated "H. Res." followed by its number, while a Senate resolution is designated "S. Res." together with its number.

Simple resolutions are considered only by the body in which they were introduced. Upon adoption, simple resolutions are attested to by the Clerk of the House of Representatives or the Secretary of the Senate and are published in the Congressional Record.

There are five statutory provisions that dictate the form of an item to be introduced in Congress, 1 U.S.C. §§ 101-105. Sections 101 and 102 dictate the exact wording of the enacting or resolving clause (the text is set out in the foregoing quote from How Are Laws Are Made). Section 103 requires that the clause enacting or resolving be in the first section of a bill or resolution. Section 104 mandates that each section of a bill or resolution be numbered and to the extent possible contain "*a single proposition of enactment.*" For an Act making an appropriation for support of the government, Section 105 specifies the exact language to be included in the title but, surprisingly, not what has to be in the body of the appropriating act.

B. STATE

The states have substantially more restrictions on the form and language of legislative proposals than the federal government. Almost all of them are in their constitutions.

Compliance with the constitutional and rule requirements is crucial for a legislative enactment to withstand a court challenge. Even though the requirements may be extremely technical, following them is mandatory.

C. CONTENT REQUIREMENTS

1. Identification and Numbering System

a. Federal

In Congress, a bill is identified by letters and numbers of the house in which it is introduced — S. for the Senate, and H.R. for the House of Representatives. Those letters are then followed by a number that indicates the order in which the bill was introduced in that session of Congress. The tenth bill introduced in the Senate is thus designated *S. 10* and the tenth bill in the House as *H.R. 10.* Correspondingly, the tenth resolution in the Senate is *S. Res. 10* and in the House *H.R. Res. 10.*

b. State

As might be expected, individual states follow a similar but not identical identification and numbering system as Congress. In Florida, for example, a bill is *S B 15* or *H B 15.* Wisconsin, on the other hand, incorporates the year in which the bill is introduced in the identification. Thus the 15th bill introduced in the year 2012 is *2012 Senate Bill 15* or *2012 Assembly Bill 15.* Usually a state's identification and numbering system is a matter of custom rather than legal requirement. Mechanically, a bill is not formally introduced until an officer or employee of the house in which the bill is filed marks it correctly. This is necessarily true as to as to its numerical designation which cannot be known in advance.

## 2.	First Words

It is the almost universal practice both in Congress and in the states that a legislative proposal start off with the words *"A Bill"* or *"A bill."* This designation may be an express constitutional mandate as in Missouri. Article III, Section 21 of its constitution states *"No law shall be passed except by bill . . . ."* Similarly, in Ohio, its Article II, Section 15A provides *"The General Assembly shall enact no law except by bill."* More states are like Tennessee where there is no express requirement for a bill, but all of the other requirements refer to a bill. Florida does not even do that, simply referring to the requirements for a *"law."*

## 3.	Title and Single Subject

Two almost-universal mandates in state constitutions are that a bill must have a title and that the bill must contain only one subject. In this context, title means a very brief description of the subject matter of the bill. The obvious purpose, of course, is to ensure that a person who looks at a bill can tell at a glance what it concerns. A typical provision is Article III, Section 6 of Florida's Constitution, which provides *"Every law shall embrace but one subject and matter properly connected therewith, and the subject shall be briefly expressed in the title."* Similarly, but in negative terms, Article II, Section 17 of Tennessee's Constitution reads *"No bill shall become a law which embraces more than one subject, that subject to be expressed in the title."* Ohio adds an additional requirement, that the title *"clearly"* express the content of bill (Article 11, Section 15(D)).

The major problem that a drafter can create in composing the title is to make it too narrow. If a bill addresses a subject matter that is beyond the scope of the words used in its title, a court could hold the enacted statute unconstitutional, as violating the descriptive title requirement. In these circumstances, the blame will fall entirely on the drafter of the bill (unless the new matter is in an amendment added after the bill is introduced).

Fortunately, the problem of the under-inclusive title is easily avoided. The key is to make the title both short and general. The longer and more descriptive the title is, the greater the chance that bill may cover a topic not included in the title. Each word added has the potential of limiting the reach of the title to the extent that it may not be fairly said to include a subject covered in the bill. Even worse, if a court finds the statute goes beyond the title, it may well declare the entire statute unconstitutional, not just the portion not described in the title. A title should thus be as general as possible but still not be so broad as to be meaningless.

For these reasons, the title of a bill raising the minimum age for obtaining a driver's license should read *"A bill relating to driver's licenses"* rather than *"A bill raising the minimum age for obtaining a driver's license from age 16 to age 17"* or *"A bill relating to the age requirement for obtaining a driver's license."* In the case of the former, if the bill were amended to raise the age to 18, the title would be incorrect and constitutionally defective. Similarly, if a bill with the latter title included a provision requiring a driver training course or eye testing for a driver over age 80, it would not withstand a constitutional challenge.

4. Enacting Clause

Whatever variations there are as to the requirements stated in sections 1-3 above, the one mandate that is almost universally present in the state constitutional provisions governing the enactment of a statute is, not surprisingly, an enacting clause. Further, the constitution usually specifies the exact language. In Florida, for example, the clause reads *"Be it enacted by the People of Florida,"* while in Georgia it is *"Be it enacted by the General Assembly of Georgia."*

If an enactment clause included in a bill varies somewhat from the precise language specified in the constitution, it is unlikely that a court would declare the statute invalid unless the word "enact" or some variation of it is not included. It is the act of enactment that converts a bill into a law. For this reason, the inclusion of some form of the word in the bill is necessary to give notice both to the members of the legislature and to the public that the legislature is engaged in law-making when it passes the bill.

(A list of the enacting clause for every state is included in Appendix A.)

5. Amendments to Existing Law

States differ as to how much of the statute being amended must appear in the bill doing the amending. Many have a provision such as Maryland's Article III, Section 29 which provides that the legislature *"in amending any article, or section of the Code of Laws of this state, to enact the same, as the said article, or section would read when amended."* This type of provision prevents the amending bill from simply providing that one word is substituted for another such as substituting age 21 for age 18. Thus a bill raising the minimum age for consuming alcoholic beverages from 18 to 21 would read *"It is unlawful for a person under age 21 to consume an alcoholic beverage as defined in section 10."* Some rules require that the words being changed be shown with a line drawn through them and the new words in some distinctive style or font. Thus the same provision would read *"It is unlawful for a person under the age of ~~18~~ **21** to consume an alcoholic beverage as defined in section 10."*

6. Municipal

There are few requirements in state law as to the content of legislation enacted by counties, cities, or other forms of local government. The one major exception is a local government operating under a home rule charter as authorized under the state constitution or statute. Either the general law or the charter may include some of the requirements applicable to state statutes such as a title or enacting clause. Because the municipal law is usually referred to as an ordinance, the enacting clause reads *"Be it ordained"* rather than *"Be it enacted."* The legal effect is, of course, the same. The first words are usually *"An Ordinance"* rather than *"A Bill."* The municipal legislative body can also adopt a resolution, but they usually do not have the same legal effect as an ordinance.

7. Examples of Bills and Ordinance

Examples of federal and state bills and a municipal ordinance follow Chapter 13.

APPENDIX A TO CHAPTER 6

State Enacting Clauses

State	Clause	Constitutional Section
Alabama	Be it enacted by the Legislature of Alabama	Art. IV, Sec. 45
Alaska	Be it enacted by the Legislature of the State of Alaska	Art. II, Sec. 13
Arizona	Be it enacted by the Legislature of the State of Arizona	Art. IV, Sec. 24
Arkansas	Be it enacted by the General Assembly of the State of Arkansas	Art. V, Sec. 19
California	The People of the State of California do enact as follows:	Art. IV, Sec. 1
Colorado	"Be it enacted by the General Assembly of the State of Colorado:"; for bills adopted by referendum, "Be it enacted by the People of the State of Colorado."	Art. V, Sec. 1, para. 8
Connecticut	Be it enacted by the Senate and House of Representatives in General Assembly convened:	Art. III, Sec. 1
Delaware	Be it enacted by the General Assembly of the State of Delaware	E.g. 78 Del. Laws 22
Florida	Be it enacted by the People of Florida	Art. III, Sec. 6
Georgia	Be it enacted by the General Assembly of Georgia	E.g. O.C.G.A. § 1-1-1
Hawaii	Be it enacted by the Legislature of the State of Hawaii	Art. III, Sec. 14
Idaho	Be it enacted by the Legislature of the State of Idaho	Art. III, Sec. 1
Illinois	Be it enacted by the People of the State of Illinois, represented by the General Assembly	Art. IV, Sec. 8
Indiana	Be it enacted by the General Assembly of the State of Indiana	Art. IV, Sec. 1
Iowa	Be it enacted by the General Assembly of the State of Iowa	Art. III, Sec. 1
Kansas	Be it enacted by the Legislature of the State of Kansas	Art. II, Sec. 20
Kentucky	Be it enacted by the General Assembly of the Commonwealth of Kentucky	Sec. 62
Louisiana	Be it enacted by the Legislature of Louisiana	Art. III, Sec. 14

State	Clause	Constitutional Section
Maine	Be it enacted by the People of the State of Maine as follows:	Art. IV, Sec. 1
Maryland	Be it enacted by the General Assembly of Maryland	Art. III, Sec. 29
Massachusetts	Be it enacted by the Senate and House of Representatives in General Court assembled, and by the authority of the same, as follows:	Ch. VI, Art. VIII
Michigan	The People of the State of Michigan enact:	Art. IV, Sec. 23
Minnesota	Be it enacted by the Legislature of the State of Minnesota	Art. IV, Sec. 22
Mississippi	Be it enacted by the Legislature of the State of Mississippi	Art. IV, Sec. 56
Missouri	Be it enacted by the General Assembly of the State of Missouri	Art. III, Sec. 21
Montana	Be it enacted by the Legislature of the State of Montana	MT Code Ann. § 5-4-101
Nebraska	Be it enacted by the people of the State of Nebraska	Art. III, Sec. 13
Nevada	The People of the State of Nevada, represented in Senate and Assembly, do enact as follows (For acts passed by popular initiative, "The People of the State of Nevada do enact as follows")	Art. IV, Sec. 23
New Hampshire	Be it Enacted by the Senate and House of Representatives in General Court convened:	Art. 92
New Jersey	Be it Enacted by the Senate and General Assembly of the State of New Jersey:	Art. IV, Sec. VII, para. 6
New Mexico	Be it enacted by the Legislature of the State of New Mexico	Art. IV, Sec. 15
New York	The People of the State of New York, represented in Senate and Assembly, do enact as follows:	Art. III, Sec. 13
North Carolina	The General Assembly of North Carolina enacts:	Art. II, Sec. 21
North Dakota	Be it enacted by the Legislative Assembly of North Dakota	Senate and House Rule 404(3)
Ohio	Be it enacted by the general assembly of the state of Ohio	Art. II, Sec. 15
Oklahoma	Be it enacted by the People of the State of Oklahoma	Okl. Const. Art. V, § 3
Oregon	Be It Enacted by the People of the State of Oregon	Bill Drafting Manual 5.7
Pennsylvania	The General Assembly of the Commonwealth of Pennsylvania hereby enacts as follows:	1 Pa. C.S. § 1101(a)

State	Clause	Constitutional Section
Rhode Island	It is enacted by the General Assembly as follows:	Art. IV, Sec. 2
South Carolina	Be it enacted by the General Assembly of the State of South Carolina	Art. III, Sec. 16
South Dakota	Be it enacted by the Legislature of the State of South Dakota	Art. III, Sec. 18
Tennessee	Be it enacted by the General Assembly of the State of Tennessee	Art. II, Sec. 20
Texas	Be it enacted by the Legislature of the State of Texas	Art. III, Sec. 29
Utah	Be it enacted by the Legislature of the State of Utah	UT Code 36-10-1
Vermont	It is hereby enacted by the General Assembly of the State of Vermont	Ch. 2, Sec. 10
Virginia	Be it enacted by the General Assembly of Virginia	E.g., 2011 Va. Acts 1
Washington	Be it enacted by the Legislature of the State of Washington	Art. II, Sec. 1, para. (d)
West Virginia	Be it enacted by the Legislature of West Virginia	Art. VI, Sec. 6-1
Wisconsin	The people of the state of Wisconsin, represented in senate and assembly, do enact as follows:	Art. IV, Sec. 17
Wyoming	Be it Enacted by the Legislature of the State of Wyoming:	Art. 21, Sec. 3

Chapter 7

ARRANGEMENT OF BILL SECTIONS

Although the order in which the sections of a bill are arranged, and in some cases their content, do not rise to the same level of the mandatory provisions described in Chapter 6[C], they are important, and the careful drafter should follow them.The drafter can find this order in the rules of the legislative body in which the bill will be introduced, or the rules may simply be customary. Whether the failure to follow them will result in invalidation of the bill as enacted is less certain than for the mandatory provisions detailed in Chapter 6, but following them will reduce the opportunities for technical challenges to it.

A. MANDATORY PROVISIONS

The initial requirements for a bill as set forth in Chapter 6[C] — identifying letters and numbers, title, and enacting clause — always come first and in that order.

B. OPTIONAL PROVISIONS

1. Short Title

Often a bill introduced in Congress will have as its first section, after the mandatory provisions, a short title that has no substantive effect but is merely a convenient way to refer to the bill after it has been enacted. For example, the health care law that was enacted in 2010 has the short title of "Patient Protection and Affordable Care Act." In many cases, the short title is simply that. Often, however, the short title is more of a political statement designed to help gain support for the bill. Few states or municipalities follow the same procedure.

2. Purpose, Policy, or Findings Statement

Another federal practice not followed in state or local governments is to include, at the beginning of a bill, a general statement as to the policy or purpose that underlies the bill. A statement like this may be simply an effort to build support for the bill or, more substantively, to influence a court in interpreting the bill after enactment. The success of the latter is dependent on the willingness of a court to look to the purpose in interpreting a specific word or section of a statute as discussed in Chapter 5.

C. IMPLEMENTING PROVISIONS

1. Placement in Existing Code

A universal requirement either in a constitutional provision, statute, legislative rule, or custom is to have a section that amends the statutory code specify the section or sections that are affected by the substantive provisions of the bill. If this is not done, it would be impossible to know by reading the bill what portion of the existing statutory law as contained in the code is being changed by it. If the bill amends an existing section of the code, the amendment can be indicated by repealing the old section and reenacting it with the new language. An even more helpful but cumbersome procedure is to show the words being changed with a line struck through them and the new words in italics or capital letters. A common requirement is for the bill to include the entire section affected, and not just the specific word or words, to show the context of the change.

It may also be necessary to add a section that repeals the section being amended to avoid the potential problem of having both simultaneously the original section and the amended section in the code. A glance at recently enacted laws of a jurisdiction will show the practice in that jurisdiction.

2. Severability

It is customary to include in a bill a clause providing that if any provision of a statute is for any reason declared invalid, the remainder of the bill is still effective. The only qualification on the severability clause is if the remainder of the bill cannot be made effective without the invalid clause, then the entire bill is invalid.

The necessity for including a severability clause is questionable. The general rule in most jurisdictions is that a court will strike down only so much of a statute that cannot be made effective without the invalid provision. Notwithstanding this general rule, most bill drafters will include a severability clause just out of an abundance of caution. The fear is that if most bills include a severability clause but one does not, the courts will conclude that the legislature intended in that one instance that if one provision in the bill is held invalid, that the whole bill should fail.

3. Saving Clause

The applicability of the bill to conduct that is subject to a penalty but which occurred prior to the statute's enactment, pending legal proceedings, or to existing legal relationships can be a problem. The general rule is that the new statute is applicable in these circumstances. To prevent this result, many jurisdictions include in their general statute governing the interpretation of statutes a provision preventing the application of the new statute to prior conduct, proceedings, or relationships, that is, from having a retroactive application. Section 8 of the Uniform Statute and Rule Construction Act provides that a statue or rule *"operates prospectively only unless the statute or rule expressly provides otherwise or its context requires that it operate retrospectively."* If the jurisdiction does not have this type of general statute, the bill drafter should ask the sponsor whether the intent is to make the bill applicable to one or more of the three situations. The bill should then specifically express the intent of the sponsor. Usually the sponsor will not have thought of the problem, although in some cases the whole purpose of the bill may be to affect what has already occurred. In this situation, the drafter will have to consider when the retroactive application of a statute is constitutionally permissible. In any event, this is a matter that the drafter should raise with the sponsor.

4. Effective Date

In most jurisdictions there is a general provision, either constitutional or statutory, that provides when a newly enacted statute becomes effective. The most common provisions are a designated calendar date such as July 1, a specified time period after approval by the executive such as 30, 60, or 90 days, or immediately upon the executive's approval.

Jurisdictions also differ on whether the effective date can be advanced or delayed. The drafter must be familiar with the applicable provision and whether an emergency provision is available. The drafter should then discuss with the sponsor whether any change from the norm is desired and legally possible.

There are occasions, however, when either because of the choice of the sponsor or the nature of the bill, the bill will have to include either temporary or phasing-in provisions. If the bill provides for a newly created body or elected or appointed official to administer it but the sponsor wants to have the law implemented immediately and not wait for the new body or official, a provision may give an existing body or official the power to administer the law until the new body or official is functional.

Another common situation is when a new multi-member body is created and the members are to have staggered terms. In this event, the bill should provide that the some of the original members have shorter terms so that after the original shorter terms have expired, the desired staggering of terms is applicable. For example, if the bill creates a 3 member commission with the members serving 3 year terms with the term of 1 member expiring each year, one of the original members will have to have a 1 year term, another a 2 year term, and the third a 3 year term. Selecting which members serve the shorter terms can be made by the appointing authority or by lot among the members. In any event, the drafter will have to include a provision directing how the staggering will be accomplished.

The drafter should put this type of provision in a separate clause that is not assigned a place in the code but is included only in the session laws. If this procedure is not followed, the temporary provision will be included in the code long after the initial shorter terms have been completed and the temporary provision has no further legal effect.

It may also be that the sponsor wants to delay the effective date of some substantive provision of the bill. A delay of this type can be important if the substantive provision requires a large and complicated administrative machinery to implement, or if the public simply needs time to adjust to the legal requirements established by the bill. In some cases, parts of the bill may be effective immediately and some later, and the bill will have to specify which sections are effective on which date.

A classic example of multiple effective dates is the federal 2010 health care reform law. The sections preventing insurance companies denying coverage of pre-existing conditions and allowing children to remain covered by their parents' insurance went into effect immediately. The individual mandate to buy health insurance, however, does not go into effect until several years later.

5. Emergency

After the substantive provisions (see section D, below) there may also be a section that provides for an earlier date for the enacted bill to go into effect than is standard, as discussed above in section 4. If the effective date is delayed, some states allow the bill to provide for an earlier effective date or to go into effect when published. In some jurisdictions, an early effective date requires passage by a super majority of each legislative chamber.

D. SUBSTANTIVE SECTIONS

The substantive sections of a bill are the heart of the bill. They make the changes in the law that affect people and what they do — impose obligations, create rights, or, as is most common, both. For this reason, they are the focus of the sponsor, the members of the legislative body that will consider the bill, the public that will be affected by it, and if administration is required, the public officials assigned that responsibility. In organizational terms, the substantive sections are divided between definitions, rights and duties, administration, and sanction or remedy. These sections are discussed in detail in Chapter 13.

E. SUBDIVISION BY LETTERS AND NUMBERS

In most jurisdictions, there is no stated requirement that establishes how a bill should be subdivided. The most common and the most helpful is a system of letters, both capital and lower case, font such as bold and italics in addition to the standard font, numbers including Arabic and Roman, i's (i.e. i, ii, iii), and parentheses (i.e. (A), (b)). These subdivision systems can usually be ascertained by checking the jurisdiction's statutory code. A drafter should never make up a special one for an individual bill. Doing so will make it impossible to draft the sections of the bill that place the those sections in the code, as described above in section [C][1].

A typical order of subdivision is:

I

II

     A.

     B.

         1.

         2.

             a.

             b.

                 (1)

                 (2)

                     (A)

                     (B)

                         (i)

                         (ii)

                             (a)

                             (b)

PART V

PRINCIPLES OF DRAFTING STATUTES AND RULES IN PLAIN ENGLISH

Chapter 8

THE EFFECT OF STRUCTURE AND STYLE ON SUBSTANCE

Writing is thinking on paper.[1]

A. TO WRITE IS TO THINK

Few individuals have made as great a contribution to our understanding of the relationship between thinking and writing, and writing and thinking, as William Zinsser, writer, editor, and Yale professor. Two of his most memorable lines are *"Writing is thinking on paper"*[2] and *"Writing and learning and thinking [a]re the same process."*[3] B.F. Skinner made the same point when he wrote *"Writing a paper is often a process of discovering what you have to say."*[4] To understand the relationship between the two is crucial to all writers but to no class of writer more than those who draft statutes or rules.

For all writers, the act of writing is the second half of the process that begins with the writer thinking about what the writer wants to say and ends with the writer choosing the precise word that most clearly expresses that thought. Writing combines a mental process — thinking, and a physical act — writing, that produces words that when joined together result in a sentence. First is the substantive thought, followed by the word choice that is intended to express that thought, one word following another that when combined convey to the reader what is in the mind of the writer.

While this thinking-writing process is intuitive and engaged in by every one who writes, it is not often understood and usually ignored. It is crucial, however, for those who write professionally to understand what they are doing so that they can enhance the quality of both their thinking and their writing. The goal is to write what they mean so that their readers can understand their intentions.

There is no class of writer for whom it is more important to be able both to think clearly and to express thoughts in easily understandable language than the statute or rule drafter. The reason for this importance is the extent of the impact that a statute or rule has on the public. A statute or rule by its nature is intended to govern the lives and actions for an indeterminable and often infinite number of people, both for the present and far into the future. No other writing except for religious books such as the

---

[1] W. Zinsser, On Writing Well 147 (1976).

[2] *Id.*

[3] W. Zinsser, Writing to Learn, Preface ix (1988).

[4] B. Skinner, *A Thinking Aid*, 20 J. of Applied Behavior 379 (1987).

Bible or Koran can affect so many people. Clarity of thought and of expressions is thus not only desirable but essential.

B. THE RELATIONSHIP BETWEEN STRUCTURE, STYLE, AND SUBSTANCE

Structured writing leads to structured thinking.

The conventional wisdom about drafting in general and statutory and rule drafting in particular is that the drafter should first concentrate on the substance, with attention given to structure and style only secondarily. Under this approach, the first goal of the drafter is to get down on paper the essential elements of the substance of the ideas of the proponent. Once that is completed, the drafter can then go back and revise the language in the draft to enhance its clarity.

The underlying premise of this book, and the reason for the authors writing it, is that this conventional wisdom is completely wrong. It is, in fact, a primary reason why most statutes and rules are so poorly drafted and thus so difficult to understand and to interpret. If writing is thinking on paper, as William Zinsser has stated so succinctly and persuasively, then the structure and style of writing used by the writer has an enormous impact on the substance contained in the writing.

What is meant by structure and style in this context is not simply sentence structure and not style in the sense of elegance. It is, rather, structure and style in the sense of knowing and following drafting principles and rules that force the drafter simultaneously to develop the substance of the statute or rule being drafted in the process of choosing both the sentence structure and the words to express the substantive thought. The discipline imposed by the drafting principles and rules set out in this book have their effect simultaneously on word choice, sentence structure, and substance. The structure of a sentence and the choice of a word not only affects the substantive choice, it is an essential part of it.

The drafter's thinking process can be disciplined or or undisciplined. The more disciplined the thought process the more likely the substantive thought produced by that process will result in a statute or rule that expresses the intent of its proponent in language that those affected by it can understand and act accordingly. The source of this discipline is contained in the drafting principles and rules as to word choice and sentence structure found in the following chapters. A statute or rule drafted in accordance with the discipline dictated by these principles will be far more likely than traditional legal writing to have the clarity that should be the goal of every statute or rule drafter.

The principles and rules that govern structure and style set forth in the following chapters are, the authors believe, the surest guide to crafting a statute or rule that most clearly expresses the intent of the statute or rule's proponent in language that can be understood both by those whose rights and duties are affected by it and by the courts that will interpret and apply it.

There are two sets of principles and rules that are the heart of the authors' approach to statute and rule drafting.

The first are the general principles and rules of Plain English drafting that are applicable to all types of legal drafting, but especially statute and rule drafting. These are contained in Chapters 10-12. The key elements of these principles and rules control the structure of each sentence written by the drafter. They can be summarized in the acronym SAPP. This stands for Singular number, Active voice, Present tense, and Positive not negative expression. It is crucial for the drafter to follow these principles and rules in every sentence.

In addition to sentence structure, the other key aspect of drafting statutes and rules in Plain English is style that determines word choice. As is noted in Chapter 1, the Plain English movement began at the end of Eighteenth Century with Jeremey Bentham's call for the use of common words in statutes. Plain English has now expanded to other aspects of word choice, including whether inclusion of a word is necessary.

The effect of style in the sense of word choice is critical to the drafting process. Each word chosen for inclusion in a statute or rule reflects a policy choice. Selecting the word that best expresses the intent of the proponent of the statute or rule and that at the same time is easily understood by anyone who reads it, from a person who may be affected by it to a court that must interpret it, is the core role of the drafter. In this way, structure, style, and substance are co-dependent, and it is this co-dependency that is the basis for the Plain English approach to statute and rule drafting.

There are special rules that apply primarily to statute and rule drafting. These are described in Chapter 13. They are not themselves part of Plain English, but control how to incorporate Plain English principles into drafting a statute or rule.

Chapter 9

THE DRAFTING PROCESS

WHAT COMES FIRST?

WHAT COMES FIRST!

It has long been a key element of the Plain English approach to legal drafting in general and statute and rule drafting in particular that the focus of the drafter should be on the *Who* and the *What* and in that order. Richard Wydick puts this principle in the following terms:

> *One way to remedy a wordy, fogbound sentence is to ask yourself: "Who is doing what to whom in this sentence?" Then rewrite the sentence to focus on those three key elements — the actor, the action, and the object of the action (if there is an object). First, state the actor. Then, state the action, using the strongest verb that will fit. Last, state the object of the action, if there is an object.*[1]

In the authors' previous writings on this subject, the the principle expressed by Wydick was characterized as concentrating on the *Who* and the *What*. The book chapters that followed were in that order. The first chapter addressed the selection and identification of the *who* — the subject of the sentence being drafted. The next chapter focused on the *what* — the predicate of the sentence that contains the action and object or complement of the action.

The authors have come to realize that while these directives fit the order in which a sentence is written, they do not fit the way in which a proponent first develops a substantive proposal that a drafter incorporates into a statute or rule. That process actually works in the reverse order.

A correct understanding of the process starts with premise that the purpose of a statute or rule is to create a legal right or or impose a legal duty. Bentham put this core principle in the following words:

> *It is by imposing obligations . . . that rights are established or granted . . . it is not possible to create rights which are not founded on obligations . . . .*

---

[1] R. Wydick, Plain English for Lawyers 15 (5th ed., 2005).

All rights rest therefore upon the idea of obligation as their necessary foundation.[2]

George Coode, writing in 1845, expressed it in the following terms:

> *The purpose of the law in all cases is to secure some benefit to some person or persons. . . . It is only possible to confer a Right, Privilege, or Power, on one set of persons by imposing corresponding Liabilities or Obligations on other persons, compelling these to afford the benefit conferred, or to abstain from invading it . . . . A law, then, can operate in two ways: it can confer the Right, Privilege, or Power directly, and it can impose the corresponding Obligation directly.*[3]

This conferring-imposition occurs almost always at the same time, because usually, when a benefit is conferred on one person, a burden is placed on someone else to grant, observe, or protect that benefit.

When the proponent of a statute or rule first conceives of a policy that requires a statute or rule to confer a benefit, impose a burden, or both, the initial thinking will address the substance of the policy favored by the proponent, e.g., texting while driving, health care, air pollution, income or sales tax. Once the proponent identifies the basic content of the substance — the *What*, the proponent will in most cases only then consider the *Who* — how broad or narrow to make the range of persons to be the subject of the *What*.

Using texting while driving as an example, the proponent will first have as a legislative objective to ban texting while driving. The proponent of that core or kernel of an idea will then have to consider what actions on what type of communications device to classify as texting and whether to make any exceptions to the banned activity. Another part of the *What* is defining driving. The proponent may want include only operating a motor vehicle for which a driver's license is required, or extend to include every type of motor or self-propelled vehicle on land, water, or in the air. Only when the proponent decides exactly what activities the statute or rule is to ban will consideration then be given to whether it should apply to all persons who engage in the banned activity or only to some such as those under or over a certain age. In any event, deciding the major outlines of the *What* will come before the *Who* — deciding to whom it should apply.

As is noted in Chapter 2, the drafter of the statute will play a major role in this entire process. In most cases, the proponent will start out only with a very rough idea of the what. It is up to the drafter to identify all of the possible options and bring them to the attention of the proponent.

This not to say, of course, that the drafter will compose the sentence or series of sentences to incorporate the *What* and the *Who* into the statute or rule in that order. As Chapter 12 indicates, the drafter will draft a sentence with a subject and predicate. Following the key principle of Plain English to write in the active rather than the

---

[2] J. Bentham, Works 181 (Bowring ed. 1843).

[3] G. Goode, On Legislative Expression: or the Language of the Written Law 6 (1845).

passive voice, the drafter will first identify the *Who* as the subject of the sentence and then the *What* as the predicate. The *What* will, however, determine the *Who* rather than the *Who* determine the *What.*

The processes of selecting the *Who* and the *What*, and the words to identify them, are not mutually exclusive. In reality they both go on at the same time. The selection of the exact parameters of the *What* will affect the the parameters of the *Who*, and vice-versa. But it all begins with the *What.*

Chapter 10

PLAIN ENGLISH PRINCIPLES ON WORD CHOICE

[E]verything which is dear to us, depends upon the choice of words. In all cases of want of precision, the fault arises either from the choice made of the words, or from the manner in which they are put together.[1]

A. USE "COMMON AND KNOWN WORDS"

It is only fitting that the very first principle ever developed for the drafting of a statute concerned word choice. Bentham set forth the following principles as practical directions for the drafting of a code of laws:

> *1. It is proper, as much as possible, not to put into a code of laws any other legal terms than such as are familiar to the people.*

> *2. If it be necessary to employ technical terms, care ought to be taken to define them in the body of the laws themselves.*

> *3. The terms of such definitions ought to be common and known words . . . .*[2]

To put it more succinctly, when drafting a statute or rule, use common (Wydick calls them familiar) words. This principle is the essence of Plain English. Those to whom a statute or rule expressly applies or may affect have the right to be able to read the statute or rule without resort to a lawyer to comprehend their rights and duties under it.

There is, of course, some debate over whether there is any standard for setting the level of education for establishing what is common and known — 8th grade or high school education, or some other standard such as being able to pass a driver's test. At the very least, the drafter should be able to assume that a reader can function in society. In today's world, that may mean being able to use a computer, search the internet, and use email. A nationally circulated newspaper such as The New York Times, USA Today, or a respected newspaper such as the Washington Post or Des Moines Register may provide a workable standard.

Another continuing debate is whether a statute or rule that regulates the conduct of only a small group or a specific industry or profession may be written in the language of that group, industry, or profession. Dickerson advocated this position. The

---

[1] J. Bentham, Works 208 (Bowring ed. 1843). The principle goes back even further. Hippocrates is quoted as saying *"The chief virtue that language can have is clarity, and nothing detracts from it so much as the use of unfamiliar words."* Abrams, *Precise, Concise, Simple and Clear*, TN Bar J., April 2011, at 14, 19.

[2] Bentham, *supra* n. 1, at 209.

major weakness of that argument is that while the specific group being regulated may be small, the beneficiaries of the regulation may be extremely broad. Examples are drug companies, banks, investment companies, health care providers, energy suppliers, developers and builders, and insurance companies. The regulations are almost invariably designed to benefit their clients or consumers. It is just as important that the latter group know the obligations of those from whom they obtain goods and services as the providers of them. For this reason, a drafter of a statute or rule should use only words understandable by the broader population.

It would serve little purpose to attempt to provide here an extensive list of common words and their less common counterparts. Examples such as buy-purchase, rent-lease, see-observe, explain-elucidate, road-thoroughfare, rich-wealthy, dig-excavate, car-automobile, duty-obligation, and poor-deprived are just a few, but they give the flavor of what is meant by common.

B. ACHIEVE BREVITY AND CLARITY BY ELIMINATING UNNECESSARY WORDS

Writing improves in direct ratio to the number of things we can keep out of it that shouldn't be there.[3]

The second key element of drafting a statute or rule in Plain English is to be brief. A drafter achieves brevity by using only so many words as are absolutely necessary to express the intent of the proponent of the statute or rule being drafted. Once again, this basic principle can be traced back to Bentham. As he put it,

Brevity of style may regard sentences and paragraphs, as well as the whole body of laws.

Lengthiness is particularly vicious when it is found in connexion with the expression of the will of the legislator.

The faults opposed to brevity which may be found . . . are —

1. Repetition in terms.

2. Virtual repetition as when the King . . . is made to say "We will, we direct, and it pleases us."

3. Repetition of specific words instead of the generic term.

4. Repetition of the definition, instead of the proper term, which ought to be defined once and for all.[4]

He went on to say that it *"is by the collection of all these defects that the English statutes have acquired their unbearable prolixity, and that the English law is smothered amidst a redundancy of words."*[5] Zinsser calls unnecessary words *"clut-*

---

[3] W. Zinsser, On Writing Well 12 (1976).

[4] Bentham, *supra* note 1, at 208.

[5] *Id.*

ter."**6**

Cutting out unnecessary or redundant words has two main advantages. The first is that the shorter the sentence, the easier it is to understand. The ultimate goal of the drafter is to achieve clarity, and shorter sentences are one of the principal ways to do that. As Strunk and White say, *"since writing is communication, clarity can only be a virtue. And although there is no substitute for merit in writing, clarity comes closest to being one."***7** They put it even more succinctly when they said *"A sentence should contain no unnecessary words. This requires . . . that every word tell."***8** Zinsser says it even more strongly: The

> *secret of good writing is to strip every sentence to its cleanest components. Every word that serves no function, every long word that could be a short word, every adverb that carries the same meaning that's already in the verb, every passive construction that leaves the reader unsure of who is doing what — these are the thousand and one adulterants that weaken the strength of a sentence. And they usually occur in proportion to education and rank.***9**

Nowhere is clarity more important than in a statute or rule because of its impact upon an unknown audience for an indefinite amount of time. If a statute or rule is to have the desired effect, a person who is subject to it must be able to read it and understand the right or duty created by it. That understanding comes from clarity, which can best be achieved by brevity.

The other principal advantage of brevity is the effect of words in a judicial proceeding involving statutory interpretation. One of the least controversial canons of statutory interpretation states that a court should attempt to give effect to each word in a statute or rule. A court can reasonably, but not necessarily, assume that each word expresses the intent of the legislature or rule maker. The court should thus attempt to discover and implement that intent. The more words in a statute or rule, the more words are subject to judicial interpretation and the more opportunities for a court to be wrong.

While brevity should always be a goal of the statute or rule drafter, clarity is the higher priority. Thus when clarity requires the inclusion of a word, the word should be added. The additional word, however, must be essential to clarity and not just the result of lazy drafting.

To eliminate clutter and achieve brevity and clarity, the drafter should focus on the words that contain the substance of each sentence — nouns, verbs, adjectives, and adverbs. These words convey the idea that the drafter is trying to express. The other types of words — articles and prepositions — on the other hand do not convey substance but merely tie together the words that do. Wydick classifies the former as working words and the latter as glue words. The fewer glue words used, the greater the brevity and clarity.

---

6 Zinsser, *supra* note 3, at 6.

7 W. Strunk & E. White, The Elements of Style 79 (4th ed., 2000).

8 *Id.* at 23.

9 Zinsser, *supra* note 3, at 6-7.

C.   USE SIMPLE RATHER THAN COMPOUND EXPRESSIONS

One of the best ways to eliminate useless words is to use simple rather than compound expressions. The compound expression is one of the types of writing that Zinsser calls clutter. A compound expression is one that reverses the good writing rule of *"don't use two words when one will do."* One theory is that the convoluted rather than simple style began when court clerks or scriveners, who later morphed into solicitors, got paid by the word for each document they prepared. Another is that this was one way a lawyer demonstrated an educational superiority over the client, similar to the use of legalese as discussed in section 4 below.

Every author who has written on good writing style and particularly Plain English has provided examples of compound expressions and their simpler counterparts. Some of the most common examples include:

compound	simple
a person is prohibited from	*a person may not*
adequate number of	*enough*
all of the	*all the*
at such time as	*when*
at that point in time	*then*
at this point in time	*now*
at the time	*when*
by means of	*by*
by reason of	*because*
by virtue of	*by*
cause it to be done	*do it, have it done*
does not operate to	*does not*
during such time as	*while*
during the course of	*during*
enter into an agreement with	*to agree with*
excessive number of	*too many*
for the duration of	*during*
for the purpose of	*to*
for the reason that	*because*
inasmuch as	*because*
in a case in which	*when (not where)*
in a prompt (or similar word) manner	*promptly*
in accordance with	*by, under*
in connection with	*with, about, concerning*
in favor of	*for*
in order to	*to*
in relation to	*about, concerning*
in the case of	*if*
in the event that	*if*

compound	simple
in the event of	*if*
in the nature of	*like, similar*
is a person who	*a person*
is able to	*can*
is applicable to	*applies*
is authorized to	*may*
is binding upon	*binds*
is directed to	*shall*
is empowered (entitled) to	*may*
is not prohibited from	*may*
is permitted to	*may*
is required to	*shall*
is unable to	*cannot*
it is directed	*shall*
it is lawful to	*may*
it is the duty of	*shall*
it is unlawful to	*may not*
or, in the alternative	*or*
paragraph 8 of subsection (c) of section 1984	*section 1984(c)(8)*
period of time	*period (time)*
prior to	*before*
provision of law	*provision*
rules and regulations	*rules*
subsequent to	*after*
sufficient number of	*enough*
the manner in which	*how*
the question as to whether	*whether*
to the effect that	*to*
under the provisions of	*under*
until such time as	*until*
used for _____ purposes	*used for _____*
with a view to	*to*
whenever	*when*
with reference to	*about, concerning*
with the object of achieving (or other gerund)	*to achieve (or other verb)*

D.   ELIMINATE LEGALESE

Probably the most common and justified criticism of legal writing is the use of what is called legalese. Legalese has no fixed definition but is usually used to describe language used by lawyers that includes words with a Latin or law French origin, circumlocutions, redundancies, and in general expressions that use uncommon words or more words than are necessary to convey the thought which the drafter seeks to express. Once again, Bentham was the first to sound the alarm against this type of writing. He did not use the term *"legalese,"* but targeted *"law jargon," "lawyers' cant,"* and *"lawyers' language."*[10] Many of the compound expressions listed in Section 3, above, are this type of writing.

The principal basis for the criticism of the use of legalese is that its use is unthinking. Usually legalese is used, not as a result of a conscious decision by the drafter that the particular word choice is the best way to express the thought the drafter seeks to express, but is simply the way the thought has been expressed in the past. Classic examples are *"last will and testament," "advise and consent,"* and *"give, devise, and bequeath,"* Sometimes they are used just because the drafter is lazy. Probably more often the drafter is concerned that a court will interpret a different or shorter expression as intending something different than what the traditional legalese has been interpreted to mean.

While the fear of the non-traditional expression may have had some justification in the past, the use of legalese in a statute or rule is no longer justified under any circumstances. The growing acceptance of the Plain English approach, and in particular in the enactment of statutes calling for its use in both statutes and rules, eliminate any possible excuse for its continued use.

E. USE THE SAME WORD TO EXPRESS THE SAME THOUGHT — THE NECESSITY FOR CONSISTENCY

One of the most important distinctions between writing in general and statute and rule drafting is the need for consistency in word choice. It is crucial for the drafter always to use the same word to convey the same thought. In other types of writing, it is thought to be desirable to vary word choice, to avoid being repetitive. This type of word choice Wydick calls *"elegant variation."*[11] The thought is that repetition is boring and that variation is interesting.

Whatever may be the literary virtues of variation, in statute and rule drafting it only invites confusion for those affected by the statute or rule or even worse for a court interpreting it. The general assumption is that when a legislative body or rule maker uses different words, it means something different.

Bentham put the rule in the following terms:

> *The same ideas, the same words. Never employ other than a single and the same word, for expressing a single and the same idea. It is, in the first place, a means of abridgment, because the explanation of the term once given, will serve for all times . . . if they vary, it is always a problem to be solved, whether it have been intended to express the same ideas, whereas, when the same words are employed, there can be no doubt but that the meaning is the*

---

[10] Mellinkoff colllects these expressions in D. Mellinkoff, The Language of the Law 263-264 (1963).

[11] R. Wydick, Plain English for Lawyers 69-70.

same. Those who are lavish of their words, know little of the danger of mistakes, and that, in legislation, they cannot be too scrupulous. The words of the laws ought to be *weighed like diamonds.*[12]

Wydick characterizes elegant variation as a language quirk.[13] In a statute or rule, it is not merely a quirk but a basic fault that can thwart the intent of the statute or rule's proponent. It is, thus, only a trap for the unwary drafter.

---

[12] J. Bentham, Works 209 (Bowring ed, 1843).

[13] Wydick, *supra* note 11, at 69-70.

Chapter 11

AMBIGUOUS AND OTHER TROUBLESOME WORDS

A. IMPORTANCE OF UNDERSTANDING WHAT TROUBLESOME WORDS ARE AND THE DIFFERENCES BETWEEN THEM

As is stated in Chapter 1, the purpose of the Plain English approach is to produce clarity in the drafting of a statute or rule. The ultimate goal is to enable the public — those who are affected by a law — to understand their rights and duties under the law. In achieving clarity, the drafter should be familiar with various words and types of words that most often create a lack of clarity in a statute or rule, either because the drafter does not understand the correct meaning of a word or uses it improperly. Dickerson describes the first three types — vagueness, generality, and ambiguity — as diseases of language.[1] This is not accurate. The problem is not in the words themselves but in their usage. The drafter can avoid them simply by using words properly. The remainder of this chapter explains how to do that.

B. AMBIGUOUS WORDS

Probably the most common criticism of a statue or rule is that it contains words that are labeled as ambiguous. The problem with these criticisms is that in many if not most cases, the critic confuses ambiguity with vagueness, generality, or some other drafting defect as discussed in section G, below.

In many cases, the criticism is unjustified or simply mislabeled. This is particularly harmful, because true ambiguity is a real problem that the statute or rule drafter must always avoid. For this reason, the statute or rule drafter needs to understand exactly what ambiguity is and how to avoid it.

While there are three types of ambiguity, the most serious and most common is syntactic. Syntactic ambiguity arises when it is unclear what a word modifies or refers back to in a statute or rule.

The first type is the *"squinty"* modifier, usually a pronoun (*when a parent is accused of abusing a child, the investigator shall interview him*). While the requirement of an interview probably applies to the parent, it could mean also mean the child. The potential for confusion is easily eliminated if the *"him"* is replaced by *"the parent"* (or *"the child"* if that is what is intended).

---

[1] R. Dickerson, The Fundamentals of Legal Drafting § 3.3 (2d. ed, 1986).

The second type occurs when a modifier precedes or follows a series of nouns (*to an employee or a contractor engaged in a hazardous activity*). Dickerson calls this type of ambiguity "semantic."[2] Here the question arises whether *"engaged in a hazardous activity"* applies to both employees and contractors engaged in hazardous activities or only to those contractors who do so. The best way to avoid confusion is to use tabulation if the modifier is intended to apply to both employees and contractors

to:

(1) an employee, or

(2) a contractor

engaged in a hazardous activity.

If intended to apply only to the last noun in the series, add a comma before that noun and add *"to"* before it and each other noun in the series (*to an employee, or to a contractor engaged in a hazardous activity*).

Another type of ambiguity Dickerson labels as semantic is the use of a word that has more than one definition. For example *"property"* can mean real, personal, tangible, or intangible property, as well as different types of ownership or possession, and different locations such as domestic or foreign. The intended meaning can sometimes but not always be determined by the context in which the word is used. This type of ambiguity is to be distinguished from homonyms — words that are spelled the same but have different meanings depending on context, e.g. *"The current issue of a financial magazine reports that corporate officers who have an issue with the SEC when it issues an order that affects a stock issue take issue with the order by challenging it in court."*

Dickerson's third type of ambiguity is contextual. This is when there are two or more meanings of a word and it is not clear which is intended. The ambiguity can be explicit or implicit, and internal or external. There is an explicit internal ambiguity one section refers to *"land"* and another to *"property"* or in one section to registering a *"vehicle"* and in another to a *"motor vehicle,"* with no apparent reason for the distinction. The explicit ambiguity is external if the same variations are in separate statutes or rules.

C. VAGUE WORDS

A vague word is one that has a broad meaning, or one that can apply to a wide range of persons or things (*corporation, resident, employee, vehicle, plant*). Unlike generality and ambiguity, the precise definition of the word determines how it should be interpreted and applied in a specific circumstance. The problem with the correct interpretation of the word is at the outer limits of the word, not at its core meaning. A word that specifies a class or category (*road, immigrant, car*), or a concept (*unlawful, unjust, democratic*) is vague but if used properly with modifiers is entirely proper and the meaning clear.

---

[2] *Id.* at § 3.4.

That is not to say that every vague word needs one or more modifiers to be used properly. It may well be that vagueness is the goal. The intentional use of a vague word is discussed in section E, below.

D.   GENERAL WORDS

A general word is one that applies to more than one thing or person. The word can mean more than one when it designates a class, e.g. *vehicle (car, truck), immigrant (legal, illegal), tree (deciduous, evergreen), plant (natural, artificial),* or *government (federal, state, local).* Generality is different from ambiguity, because it allows simultaneous reference, while ambiguity can have only alternative reference. A general word can be over-inclusive or under-inclusive, so the careful drafter must be very precise, especially through the use of modifiers, to avoid both.

E.   THE DIFFERENCES BETWEEN VAGUE AND GENERAL WORDS

As sections B and C, above, demonstrate, vague and general words are not mutually exclusive because each type includes classes of persons, things, or actions. The statute or rule drafter must be careful to distinguish between them by selecting the precise word and modifiers that most clearly reflect the drafter's intent. The exact differences are:

A vague word can be:

   a. *a concept* — *justice, balanced, equality, fairness, poor, rich;*

   b. *an adjective* — *near, intentional, material, adjacent, high, low, handi-capped, impaired, injured, reasonable;*

   c. *an action* — *run, donate, advise, request, offer, harm, help, urge, promote.*

A general word is a noun that includes a class that is comprised of persons or things — *son, daughter, employee, lover, state, country, gift, hazard, crime, horse, cat, garage, shed.*

F.   INTENTIONAL USE OF A VAGUE OR GENERAL WORD

The careful statute or rule drafter may intentionally use a vague or general word, but only under limited circumstances when that is the intent of the proponent of the statute or rule being drafted. For the proponent, the intent may be purely political in attempting to gloss over objections to the statute or rule if its application under various circumstances were known in advance.

The proponent may also be uncertain how and under what circumstances the statute or rule should be applied in the future. In that case, the proponent may want to let the court or agency that will apply the statute or rule make that determination, being guided only by the vague or general words used in the statute or rule. This tactic is particularly appropriate when general concepts such as due process or equal protection are used, because their meaning can evolve over the passage of time.

As can be seen from the discussion of ambiguous words in the next sections, an ambiguous word should never be used intentionally.

G. CONFUSING AMBIGUITY WITH OTHER TYPES OF POOR DRAFTING

It is unfortunate that in some of the otherwise valid criticisms of the quality of the drafting of statutes and rules, there has been a tendency to mislabel many drafting deficiencies as ambiguities, when in fact they are another type. One critic listed words such as "reasonable" and "due process" as ambiguous even though, as is shown above, these words are not ambiguous but vague (and properly so).[3] In the same manner, a federal committee listed a series of recommendations for eliminating what it called statutory ambiguities.[4] In fact, all but one of them involved only statutes that should have addressed a problem but did not, while the last addressed the failure to define key terms. None involved ambiguity.

Adding to the confusion was an article reviewing the study committee's report. The author examined U.S. Supreme Court decisions interpreting several federal statutes. He claimed that there were 20 repeated ambiguities in statutes interpreted by the Court.[5] The reality is that 17 of the so-called ambiguities involved only the failure of a statute to address an issue, while the others concerned general or vague terms. None was an ambiguity problem.

Obviously, ambiguity in a statute or rule is a problem. Mislabeling a drafting error such as using a vague or general term or the failure to include a necessary provision as an ambiguity will not help eliminate ambiguities, but only compound the problem.

H. HOW TO ELIMINATE AMBIGUITY, UNINTENDED VAGUENESS, AND OVER AND UNDER GENERALITY

Being aware of the difficulties that can be caused by ambiguity, unintended vagueness, or over or under generality is the first step for the statute or rule drafter but not the last. For ambiguity, the best way to eliminate most forms of it is to use the drafting principles and rules set forth in this book, especially Chapters 10-13. Using the singular number, active voice, and the present tense, and gender neutral drafting will do wonders in eliminating syntactic ambiguity. Following good drafting techniques, however, cannot eliminate unintended vagueness and over or under generality. Rather, their elimination requires the statute or rule drafter to know the intention of the proponent for whom the drafting is being done, being conscious of the consequences of using the wrong word, and being precise in choosing the correct word. In other words, statute and rule drafting require the highest degree of drafting skill.

---

[3] Miller, *Statutory Language and the Purposive Use of Ambiguity*, 42 Va. L. Rev. 39 (1956).

[4] Federal Courts Study Committee, Final Report 155-56 (1990).

[5] Maggs, *Reducing the Costs of Statutory Ambiguity*, 29 Harv. J. on Legislation 123, 143-48 (1998).

I. COMMONLY MISUSED WORDS AND PHRASES

1. *"No Person Shall," "Shall Not,"* **and** *"This Act (section) Shall Not Be Construed to"*

Few phrases are used more often in the drafting of not only statutes and rules but constitutions than *"no person shall"* and *"shall not."* Perhaps the biggest user (or misuser) is the U.S. Constitution, which loves the variant *"no state shall."*

Both are used for the same purpose — to prohibit a government or person from doing something. The only problem is that neither is the proper way to express the prohibition. The proper way to do so is discussed in Chapter 12.

The phrase *"This Act (section) shall not be construed"* is even worse, because it combines the passive voice, a misuse of *"shall,"* and a direction as to statutory interpretation, all in one short phrase. A statute or rule drafter should never use it. The better way to express the same idea is to state the legal rule as just that. Thus a provision that reads *"This section shall not be construed to require prescription drug coverage"* should read *"An insurer may offer a plan that does not cover prescription drugs."*

2. *Assure, Ensure, and Insure*

The words *"assure," "ensure,"* and *"insure"* create difficulty in everyday use as well as in drafting a statute or rule. To ensure proper usage, to assure the client for whom the statute or rule is drafted accurately expresses the intent of the client, and to insure against misinterpretation of the statute or rule by the public and the courts, the drafter must understand what each of the three words means and when to use one rather than the others. (Note to the reader — the foregoing sentence uses each of the three words correctly).

The easiest way to understand when to use *"assure"* is understand that the word always requires a person, either expressed or implied, as the object. To assure is to give an assurance of something, to create confidence in the person receiving the assurance. In daily usage, *"reassure"* is often used to express the same meaning as *"assure"* even though there is usually no earlier assurance that is being re-enforced. *"Reassure"* is always used with a person as the object and *"assure"* should be used the same way. If the drafter uses *"assure"* in any other way, the use is incorrect.

In most instances, when a person uses the word *"assure"* or *"insure,"* what the person means is *"ensure,"* that is to make certain. (*To ensure sufficient funding for the project, the county shall impose a tax on real property sufficient for that purpose.*) The simplest way to use *"insure"* correctly in drafting a statute or rule is to use it only when referring to taking out insurance, such as property, health, or life insurance, or some other type of effort to mitigate loss or misuse. The distinction can be seen in the following examples: (*To ensure repayment of the loan, the borrower shall post collateral that exceeds the amount of the loan; The borrower shall insure the mortgaged property against physical loss for the amount of the mortgage*).

3. *Share*

A recent phenomenon in the use and misuse of language is the word *"share."* In the past decade the word has gone from being used to mean the dividing up of a tangible (a cake) or intangible (ownership) item to being a substitute for various words that mean the providing of information (*tell, report inform, relate*). Instead of telling someone something, you share it with them. One story, perhaps apocryphal, concerns Chief Justice Rehnquist of the U.S. Supreme Court and a lawyer arguing a case before the Court. The lawyer began by saying the he would share the facts of the case with the Court. The Chief Justice interrupted, saying *"Never mind sharing them, just tell us what they are."*

In a statute or rule, it would be incorrect to say that *"an applicant shall share with the agency the purposes for which the funds are sought."* Instead, the statute or rule should require that *"an applicant shall state in detail the purposes for which the funds are sought."*

4. *Only*

"Only" is another word that is misused in every day usage even more often than in drafting a statute or rule, but the effect is seldom as serious. The problem with *"only"* is different from other troublesome words in that the problem is one of placement, not of definition. The following example concerning the firing of an employee demonstrates the problem:

Only an employer may terminate an employee for cause.

An employer only may terminate an employee for cause.

An employer may only terminate an employee for cause.

An employer may terminate only an employee for cause.

An employer may terminate an employee only for cause.

As can be seen from these examples, there are five possibilities for the placement of *"only."* Only the fifth one accurately states the correct rule — cause is required to terminate an employee. It is just as likely, however, that third example will be used with *"only"* placed before *"terminate."* This wording, however, suggests that termination is the only possible penalty, excluding a lesser penalty such as suspension, docking or reduction in pay, transfer, or reduction in grade or position. In almost all instances, this is not what would be intended. The simple rule to be followed with *"only,"* as with all modifiers as is discussed in Chapter 12[C][1], is to place it as close as possible to the word it modifies. In the above example, the restriction applies to *"for cause,"* and thus it should be placed as close as possible to those words. That is what is done in the fifth example.

Chapter 12

PLAIN ENGLISH PRINCIPLES AND RULES ON DRAFTING A SENTENCE

There isn't any thought or idea that can't be expressed in a fairly simple declarative sentence, or in a series of fairly simple declarative sentences.[1]

A. BASIC PRINCIPLES

1. The Simple Declarative Sentence — The Drafter's Best Friend

For the drafter of a statute or rule, the most basic advice on writing is the best — use the simple declarative sentence as the building block for the statute or rule. In each sentence, there is a subject and a predicate. The subject is a noun, the predicate is a verb, and the object or complement of the verb. Put them together, sentence after sentence, and the result is a statute or rule that expresses the intent of the proponent of the statute or rule in language that can be understood by those who are governed by it, i.e., the public.

It is not a coincidence that E.B. White (best known as the co-author of the most famous book on good writing, *The Elements of Style*) was prompted to make the comment quoted above concerning the virtues of the simple declarative sentence by a sentence on the federal income tax Form 1040. That sentence listed income items partially exempt from the tax. The listing included three parenthetical phrases[2] that caused White to make the following comment:

> *I want to ask my government what it thinks would become of me and my family if I were to write like that! Three sets of parentheses in one sentence! I would be on relief inside of a month.*

> *That sentence, above, was obviously written by a lawyer in one of his flights of rhetorical secrecy. There isn't any thought or idea which can't be expressed in a fairly simple declarative sentence, or in a series of fairly*

---

[1] E. White, One Man's Meat 133 (1944). William Zinsser put it this way: *"What does preoccupy me is the plain declarative sentence. How have we managed to hide it from so much of the population?"* Writing to Learn 10 (1988).

[2] *"Amounts received (other than amounts paid by reason of death of the insured and interest payments on such amounts and other than amounts received as annuities) under a life insurance or endowment contract, but if such amounts (when added to amounts received before the taxable year under such contract) exceed the aggregate premiums or consideration paid (whether or not paid during the taxable year) then the excess shall be included in gross income . . . ."* White, *supra* n. 1, at 133.

simple declarative sentences. The contents of Section G of Form 1040, I am perfectly sure, could be stated so that the average person could grasp it without suffering dizzy spells. I could state it plainly myself if I could get some lawyer to disentangle it for me first. I'll make my government a proposition: for a five-dollar bill (and costs) I **will** *state it plainly.*[3]

To some, especially the critics of Plain English, the approach that relies on common words and basic sentence structure is too simple. For them, statutes and rules are complicated matters, usually dealing with specialized areas of human activity and addressed to specialists in those areas. For this reason, statutes and rules can be both complicated in word choice and in structure, leaving it to the experts to figure out how to interpret and apply them.[4]

The authors' experiences in both drafting and interpreting statutes and rules, and in teaching how to do both, persuades them that the advocates of Plain English have much the better of the argument. All one need do is look at the output of almost all legislative and rule making bodies to see the validity of the Plain English movement and why it is growing in acceptance on a daily basis. Its principles are nothing new. They can be traced back to the principles laid down by Jeremey Bentham over two centuries ago. The only change in the interim has been the growth in the number of laws that regulate our society, especially in statutes and rules.

2. Use Short Sentences

Proposition: The shorter the sentence the better. Rule: Minimize the length of sentences.[5]

The originator of Plain English, Jeremey Bentham, recognized the virtue of using short sentences in a statute or rule as a key feature of drafting understandable laws when he wrote the sentence quoted above at the end of the 18th century. For him, as it has been with his successors, the short sentence is at the heart of both clarifying the thinking of the drafter during the drafting process and the reader's comprehension at the end of the law making process.

Bentham did not only state the rule in favor of short sentences, he gave the reasons behind it in the following words:

1. The shorter the sentence, the clearer is it to the eyes of the reader; — the clearer, that is to say, the more free from obscurity — . . . the more easily retained in the memory.

2. The shorter the sentence, the clearer it is in the eyes of the legislator and the judge.[6]

---

[3] *Id.*

[4] See the discussion in Chapter 1[D].

[5] J. Bentham, Works 264 (Bowring ed., 1843).

[6] *Id.*

William Zinsser expressed the same advice: *"There is no minimum length of sentence that's acceptable in the eyes of God. Among good writers it is the short sentence that predominates . . . ."*[7]

Rudolph Flesch, one of the first Americans to urge lawyers to use Plain English, especially in administrative rules, developed a readability formula. This formula, which he developed in the early 1940s, was based on two factors — length of sentences and length of words. As he put it, the

> *"longer the sentence, the more ideas your mind has to hold in suspense until its final decision of what all the words mean together. Longer sentences are more likely to be complex — more subordinate clauses, more prepositional phrases and so on . . . . So the longer a sentence, the harder it is to read."*[8]

What these authors are trying to tell the drafter is to put only one thought or idea in each sentence. The trap that many drafters of statutes and rules fall into is to think that if the basic legal proposition in a statute or rule is subject to qualifications as to the persons or circumstances addressed by it, the drafter should include those qualifications in the original sentence rather than in additional short sentences. One justification for doing so is a fear that a reader, and particularly a judge, may overlook or ignore the qualification if it is not contained in the same sentence of the legal rule it is qualifying. This fear has no legal basis and should not be an argument for one long sentence rather than a series of short sentences.

B.   GENERAL RULES ON CRAFTING THE SUBJECT AND PREDICATE

In crafting a short, simple declarative sentence, the acronym SAPP summarizes the four key rules to follow in doing so. They are to use the:

S — Singular (not plural) number

A — Active (not passive) voice

P — Present (not future) tense

P — Positive (not negative) form

1.   Make the Subject a Singular Rather Than a Plural Noun

As is stated in Chapter 9, the purpose of a statute or rule is to confer a right or impose a duty (recognizing that doing one automatically does the other). Use of the simple declarative sentence as the vehicle for doing either, and use of the active voice as set out in section 2, below, demand that the person who receives the right or duty be the subject of the sentence. The sentence should thus start with a noun that identifies that person.

---

[7] W. Zinsser, On Writing Well 71 (1976).

[8] R. Flesch, How to Write Plain English 22 (1979).

The first rule that governs the selection of the noun is to use the singular rather than the plural. While this rule seems simplistic, the fact is that historically, most statutes and rules use a plural rather than a singular noun to identify the persons covered by them. The reason behind the preference for the plural was probably the fear that if the singular rather than the plural was used, the statute or rule might be interpreted to apply to only one person rather than all those who fit within the definition of the noun. It was for this reason that most jurisdictions adopted a statute that provided that use of the singular included the plural and vice-versa.

There are, in fact, several good reasons to use the singular rather than the plural for the noun that is the subject of the sentence. Most important, the singular emphasizes that the right or duty created by the sentence applies to each member of the affected class individually, not just collectively. Further, it is easier to understand the impact of the sentence if it is cast in terms of a particular person than simply the group to which the person belongs. Lastly, consistent use of the singular eliminates any unintentional inconsistencies between singular and plural in using the same noun, pronoun, verb, object, or complement in the same or a subsequent sentence.

2. Use the Verb in the Predicate in the Active Rather Than Passive Voice

If there is any rule of Plain English that can be described as the most important and at the heart of drafting clear and simple statutes and rules, it is the rule that calls for the use of a verb in the active rather than the passive voice. In the context of the principle that the purpose of a statute or rule is to create a right or impose a duty, then its core language will read either *a person (or other entity) may* to create a right or *a person (or other entity) shall* or *may not* to impose a duty. This format requires identification of the person or entity benefited or burdened and forces choosing the noun for the subject of the sentence. Once the drafter adopts this approach to crafting each sentence in a statute or rule, almost every other aspect of Plain English falls into place. More than anything else, the active voice keeps the focus of the drafter on the principal task of creating a right or imposing a duty.

3. Put the Verb in the Present Rather Than the Future Tense

Tense when used in the context of grammar means time of action — past, present, or future. Thus a sentence with a transitive verb (one that requires an object) such as "*apply*" can provide that a person has applied for a permit in the past, applies for one in the present, or shall or will apply for one in the future. Similarly an intransitive verb (one that is followed by a complement) such as "*is*" can provide that a person *was, is,* or *shall be* eligible to do something.

A chronic problem of statutory and rule drafting has been for the drafter to think only in terms of the future because the provision being drafted will be effective only in the future. Thus it has been most common for statutes and rules to be filled with *shalls.* In many if not most instances, the use of *shall* is not to impose a duty on someone but merely to describe what will occur in the future.

To avoid the confusion created by the use of *shall* both for the purpose of imposing a duty and indicating the future, the drafter should always keep in mind the basic legal principle that a statute or rule always speaks in the present. This means that when a court or administrative agency seeks to determine the applicability of the statute or rule to the facts in the proceeding before it, the statute or rule is contemporaneous with those facts. To have the statute or rule written in the language of the future only causes confusion of the issue and requires the court or agency to make a mental transition from the future tense of the statute or rule to the present tense of the facts established in the proceeding before it. The best way to avoid the confusion is to draft the statute or rule in the present tense.

4.   Use the Finite Verb Rather Than Its Noun Version

One of the simplest ways to write clearly and simply is to use the finite verb (*to speak, to apply, to pay*) rather than converting the verb into a noun (*to give a speech, to submit an application, to make a payment*). Lawyers are notorious for engaging in this practice for the same inexplicable reasons that gave rise to the Plain English movement. Dickerson called the finite verb a live word and distinguished it from the variations of it as participles, gerunds, nouns, and adjectives.[9] Wydick distinguishes between base verbs and nominalizations.[10] They are both referring to the same bad habit — using the indirect and lengthier expression rather than the direct and shorter expression. Under Flesch's word and syllable system for testing readability, the finite or base verb always wins out.[11] (*The Secretary may authorize* rather than *The Secretary may issue an authorization to.*) There is simply no justification for using any other of its forms.

5.   Draft the Sentence in the Positive Rather Than the Negative Form

Many if not most sentences that a drafter includes in a statute or rule can be put in the positive or negative form. Thus a sentence concerning age eligibility can be drafted to read "*a person age 18 or over and otherwise qualified may vote in an election*" or "*a person age 18 or over and not otherwise disqualified may vote in an election.*" The first sentence is in the positive, the second in the negative. The problem with the second is that it has a double negative — *not otherwise disqualified* — which makes the sentence both longer and more difficult to understand.

A double negative can usually be identified when the negative *not* is used with a negative word such as one that begins with letters that suggests the negative such as *in (ineligible)*, *un (unqualified)*, or *dis (disqualified)* or words that are negative in effect such as *eliminate, strike, impaired,* or *fail.*

---

[9]   R. Dickerson, Fundamentals of Legal Drafting § 8.9 (2d ed., 1986).

[10]   R. Wydick, Plain English for Lawyers 23-24 (5th ed., 2005).

[11]   Flesch, *supra* note 8, at ch. 2.

6. Follow the Verb With an Object or Complement

The second part of the predicate is what follows the verb. The verb can be transitive, that is one that shows action on someone or something (*the secretary may appoint a deputy, the secretary shall issue guidelines*). It can also be intransitive, that is, has no receiver of an action but establishes a relationship with the noun in the subject. The most common use in a statute or rule is to establish a right or eligibility or declare a status (*a resident may (is eligible to) vote, an employee may (is eligible to) retire, January 1 is a holiday, a state sales tax is deductible*).

C. FURTHER RULES TO AID CLARITY

1. The Subject

a. Identifying the Subject

The combination of the basic rules that call for the use of the singular noun as the subject of the sentence and an active verb in the predicate requires that the subject of the sentence be a person who is either the recipient of a right or has a duty to act or not act.

If the statute or rule has universal application to everyone, the best designation is "a person." This term includes both natural persons and all other entities, both natural and artificial. The 1995 Uniform Statute and Rule Construction Act in section 3(3) defines "person" as follows:

> *"Person" means an individual, corporation, business trust, estate, trust, partnership, limited liability company, association, joint venture, [government, governmental subdivision, agency, or instrumentality,] or any legal or commercial entity.*

The U.S. Code has a similar but not identical provision in 1 U.S.C. § 1, and most states do likewise. The careful drafter will check the applicable law in the jurisdiction for which the statue or rule is being drafted to ensure the particular entity which is the subject of the statute or rule is included in the definition of *person*. If not, the drafter will have to define the term or use a special term that encompasses the entity the drafter wants to include in the reach of statute or rule.

All of the foregoing applies only if the statute or rule is intended to be of universal application. If the application is to be limited to only a particular class, such as minors, females, partnerships, students, or motor vehicle operators, the drafter must use the precise term that includes all of those the statute or rule's proponent wants to cover, but only those. That may require a special term and definition, depending on other statutory or rule provisions in the relevant jurisdiction. Special rules for definitions are discussed in Chapter 13[B].

b.   Use an Article Rather Than an Adjective as the Subject's Modifier

A common mistake in statute and rule drafting that is as old as the activity is to use an indefinite adjective such as *any, each, every,* or *no* to refer to the subject or the object or complement of the verb in a sentence. A common expression in the U.S. Constitution is *no person shall.* Also common both in the Constitution and in federal and state statutes and rules are references to *any, each, every,* or *no* person, state, bill, or other noun that is the subject or object of the sentence.

Apparently, this drafting preference stemmed from a fear that if the articles *a* or *an* were used, a court may think that it was a substitute for the adjective *one,* thus making the applicability of the statute limited to only one person or thing. In most instances, these problems are avoided by a general rule of construction that provides that the singular includes the plural.

Dickerson suggested the following rules:[12]

(1) If a right, privilege, or power is conferred, use "any" (e.g., "Any qualified state officer may").

(2) If an obligation to act is imposed, use "each" (e.g., "Each qualified state officer shall").

(3) If a right, privilege, or power is abridged, or an obligation to abstain from acting is imposed, use "no" (e.g., "No qualified state officer may").

Notwithstanding Dickerson's many contributions to the improvement of legal drafting and legislative drafting in particular, in this case, the statute or rule drafter should not follow his advice. In each of his examples, there is no difference in the legal effect of saying *a qualified state officer may, shall,* or *may not* do something than using *any, each,* or *no.* The articles *a* or *an* cover them all. If, of course, the intent is to limit the applicability of the sentence to fewer than all persons or things, then a specific number (*one, ten*) or some other limit (*as many as are authorized*) should be used.

An even worse use of an adjective rather than an article to modify a noun is the classic legalese words *such* and *said* to refer to a noun used earlier in the statute or rule (*A driver's licence may be revoked if said/such driver is convicted of*). There is no need for these pretentious words. The Plain English article *the* will in every instance serve the same purpose (*A driver's license may be revoked if the driver is convicted of*).

Such may be appropriate when it is used with *as* to introduce a list of options or variables as an alternative to the word *including* (*An applicant may demonstrate qualifications for the position such as education, work experience, or on the job training*).

---

[12]   Dickerson, *supra* note 9, at § 9.5.

c. Minimize Use of Pronouns

Chapter 11 on Ambiguous and Other Troublesome Words in section B discusses the problem of ambiguity. As that chapter points out, one of the most common types of ambiguity is syntactic. This is the type of ambiguity that results from uncertainty of what a word refers to in a prior clause or sentence in a statute or rule. This type of ambiguity occurs most often when the second term is a pronoun (*If the driver and a passenger are each injured in an accident, he shall report the accident to his insurance carrier*). In the first clause there are two nouns, *driver and passenger*, and two pronouns in the second clause, *he* and *his*. While it is likely that both pronouns refer to the driver, another possible interpretation is that the obligation to report is on the passenger. If so, it is unclear whether the passenger should report to his or the driver's insurance carrier. All of this confusion can be eliminated if the pronouns are replaced by nouns (*If the driver and a passenger are each injured in an accident, the driver shall report the accident to the driver's insurance carrier*) or at least by eliminating the first pronoun *he* (*the driver shall report the accident to his insurance carrier*).

A second problem with the use of pronouns is that they are often masculine or feminine (*he, she, his, hers*). The problem used to be dealt with by a provision in a jurisdiction's statutory rules of interpretation that mandated in the words of Section 5(b) of the 1995 Uniform Statute and Rule Construction Act "[*u*]*se of a word of one gender includes corresponding words of the other genders.*" This approach is no longer acceptable, because almost all jurisdictions now require that statutes and rules be drafted in gender neutral terminology.

The most common and usually the easiest way to avoid the sexist pronoun is to repeat the noun rather than use a pronoun. That is the technique used in the example above in repeating the word *driver* rather than using the pronouns *he* and *his*. Another is to use a gender neutral term rather than a sexist one, e.g., *spouse* rather than *husband* or *wife*, *person* rather than *man*, *parent* rather than *husband* or *wife*. It may also be possible to simply omit the pronoun if the meaning remains clear (*A defendant shall enter a plea when arraigned* rather than *A defendant shall enter a plea when he is arraigned*).

There are some words that historically had masculine and feminine counterparts such as *actor/actress, waiter/waitress, aviator/aviatrix, host/hostess, heir/heiress* even though the masculine term did not inherently suggest male rather than female. In these cases, there is no reason not to use the term that was previously used as the masculine. Another is to convert words that included the words *man* or *men* such as *draftsman, salesman*, or *workman* or their plural versions and use *drafter, sales clerk*, or *worker*.

It may also be possible to use the gender neutral pronoun *it* when the noun it is used to substitute for includes both natural and artificial persons. These include *buyer, seller, owner, agent, defendant, party, publisher, representative, sender, payor*, and other similar words.

Less satisfactory proposals are to use *he or she*, or even worse *he/she*, the plural *they* or *their*, or attach *person* as in *draftperson* or *waitperson*.

2. The Predicate

a. The Verb

i. Place the Negative With the Verb in the Predicate Rather Than With the Noun in the Subject

There are few expressions more common in constitutions, statutes, and rules than the negative command that begins with the phrase *"No person shall"* (or with its equivalent addressed to the particular object of the prohibition such as *person, State, taxpayer, defendant, employer, agent, officer, or agency*). As Dickerson correctly points out, this form of negative grammatically does not accomplish what it attempts to do, that is prohibit someone from doing something. All that it does is state that no one is obligated to perform the act that is sought to be prohibited.[13]

Dickerson's solution is to have the prohibition start with *"No person may."*[14] This is not a satisfactory solution. It continues the same weakness of the traditional *"No person shall"* in that it is not addressed to any specific person or class of persons. The intent is, of course, just the opposite — it is addressed to every person who is a member of the class within the prohibition.

The easiest and most direct, and thus the clearest, way to impose a prohibition is to put the prohibition in the verb. This means that the sentence should begin with a noun that includes all of those sought to be prohibited from doing something (*a person, State, taxpayer, defendant, employer, agent, officer, or agency*). That noun should be followed by the negative verb *may not*, which in turn is followed by the type of action that is prohibited. (*A driver may not exceed the posted speed limit.*)

Another rule comes into play in stating a negative — the rule that a provision should be stated in positive rather than the negative whenever possible. Thus a statute or rule that establishes a time period for taking an action should provide that the act must be done within the time limit (*An appellant shall file its brief within 30 days of the filing of the record*) not that it may not be done after the time period (*An appellant may not file its brief more than 30 days after the filing of the record*). The former is clearer, more direct, and shorter and thus much to be preferred.

The phrase *"This Act (section) shall not be construed"* is even worse because it combines the passive voice, a misuse of *"shall,"* and a direction as to statutory interpretation all in one short phrase. A statute or rule drafter should never use it. The better way to express the same idea is to state the legal rule as just that. Thus a provision that reads *"This section shall not be construed to require an insurer to offer nursing home care"* should read *"An insurer may offer a plan that does not cover nursing home care."*

---

[13] Dickerson, *supra* note 8, at § 9.4.

[14] *Id.*

ii.   Use *"May"* to Create a Right or to Grant Authority or Discretion

As noted in Chapter 9, Bentham and Goode pointed out long ago, the central function of a statute (and now a rule) is to confer a right or impose a duty. Traditionally, this was done by the use of the word *shall* as is discussed in the next section. Far better is to use the word *may* (*The President may reorganize an executive department; The Supreme Court may adopt rules of procedure; An employee may retire at age 65; A taxpayer may claim a refund*).

To impose a condition on the exercise of the right, authority, or discretion, it is misleading to say *a taxpayer shall file a claim for a refund within one year of the overpayment* because that suggests there is an obligation to file the claim, thus creating a false imperative. The proper way to express the limitation is to use an introductory clause (*To seek a refund, a taxpayer shall file a claim within one year of the overpayment; Before a proposed rule becomes effective, the Supreme Court shall file the rule with the legislature at least 30 days before the effective date*).

b.   Use *"Shall"* to Require an Action

As discussed in Chapters 11[H][1] and 12[G], few words are used incorrectly in statutes and rules more often than *shall*. Most often the word is used in the future tense (*If a person shall file a claim*) but also in other instances such as imposing a prohibition (*a person shall not*) or creating a false imperative (*a person shall have a claim, the record shall consist of*). Given its importance in establishing legal duties, its use in any other context can only create confusion and weaken its effect when used properly.

To create a duty to act in a simple declarative sentence with a singular noun and an active verb, the sentence will read: *The clerk shall open the office during normal business hours each weekday that is not a public holiday; The governor shall submit a budget to the Legislature by January 15; A driver arrested for a violation shall submit to a breathalyzer test; An applicant shall provide the information in the form requested by the employer; A passenger shall provide a government issued identification that includes a photograph of the passenger.*

Not all of these obligations are the same. In the case of the clerk, the obligation to open the office is ministerial and can be enforced by a writ of mandamus. In the case of the governor submitting a budget, because the preparation of a budget involves the use of discretion, a court could not enforce the obligation, making the duty enforceable only by political means such as impeachment. The obligation of the driver who is arrested to take a breathalyzer test can be enforced by the criminal law with either a revocation of license, fine, or jail sentence.

With regard to the applicant submitting information or the passenger providing a photo ID, these are not absolute duties but only duties that arise out of voluntary action that can be abandoned by the person upon whom the duty is imposed. It is, thus, only a conditional duty. A requirement that relates to the exercise of a right, particularly a constitutional one such as voting, is in a different category. Some states now require a photo ID for voting. This requirement is not merely conditional, because it pertains to something a person has a right to do. A law may impose this type of condition only if is not considered an undue burden on a constitutional right.

3.   Rules Applicable to Both Subject and Predicate

a.   Place a Qualifier Before the Subject or After The Predicate and as Close as Possible to the Word Modified

One of the most common ways in which drafter can make a statute or rule difficult to read and understand is to place qualifying language, usually a clause containing several words, between the subject (a noun) and predicate (a verb and an object or complement). This sentence structure creates confusion because it separates the key elements of the statute or rule — the subject and the predicate — from language that modifies one or the other.

The best way to overcome this potential confusion is to place the qualifier either at the beginning or end of the sentence or in a separate sentence. If the qualifier relates to the subject and is included in the same sentence, it should come at the beginning of the sentence. If it relates to the predicate, it should come at the end of the sentence. Put another way, it should be placed as close as possible to the word that it qualifies. Often the best way is to put the qualifier in a separate sentence that follows the sentence which it is qualifying.

Section 2284(b)(3) of 28 U.S.C. relating to three judge district courts gives several examples of how not to provide for qualifiers. The subsection reads as follows:

> *A single judge may conduct all proceedings except the trial, and enter all orders permitted by the rules of civil procedure except as provided in this subsection. He may grant a temporary restraining order on a specific finding, based on evidence submitted, that specified irreparable damage will result if the order is not granted, which order, unless previously revoked by the district judge, shall remain in force only until the hearing and determination by the district court of three judges of an application for a preliminary injunction. A single judge shall not appoint a master, or order a reference, or hear and determine any application for a preliminary or permanent injunction or motion to vacate such an injunction, or enter judgment on the merits . . . .*

The first sentence includes an exception at the end of the sentence. Since the exceptions referred to are contained in the subsection, there is no reason to refer to the exception.

The second sentence has four qualifiers. The first requires that a temporary restraining order be based on a specific finding of irreparable harm if the order is not issued, that the finding be based on evidence submitted, and that the order remain in effect until revoked by the judge or until the hearing and ruling on the injunction by the three judge panel.

The first two qualifiers relating to the requirements for a temporary restraining order should be combined and stated first *"Upon evidence submitted that a specified irreparable harm will occur, the judge may issue a temporary restraining order."*

The last two qualifiers governing how long the TRO remains in effect should be stated in a separate sentence reading *"The order remains in effect until the judge revokes it or the three judge court rules on the application for a preliminary injunction."*

The entire quoted subsection would then read:

> *A single judge may conduct all proceedings except the trial and enter all orders permitted by the rules of procedure. Upon evidence submitted that a specified irreparable harm will occur, the judge may issue a temporary restraining order. The order remains in effect until the judge or three judge court revokes it or the three judge court rules on an application for a preliminary injunction. The single judge may not appoint a master, order a reference, hear or grant an application for or to vacate a preliminary or permanent injunction, or enter judgment on the merits . . . .*

One of the worst features of the traditional form of a statute was the use of the proviso. Under this format, a qualifier would be added to the end of the original sentence beginning with the words *"provided that"* followed by the qualifying language. This format was often used when the statute was amended either when originally considered or by a subsequent statute. Usually, it was the simplest way to make an amendment even if it made the statute more difficult to understand. The practice became so common that further amendments were made by adopting language that began with the words *"provided further that."*

George Coode in the mid-19th century became the most prominent advocate of eliminating the proviso clause,[15] but its use has continued to the present. For example, 28 U.S.C. § 2415(a) requires that the United States bring an action for money damages based on a contract within six years of the accrual of the action. It then has four qualifications to the six year limit, each following a colon and beginning with the words *Provided* or *Provided further.* The entire section is one sentence and contains 370 words, making it almost impossible to understand without breaking the sentence down into its component parts. Even worse, the section starts out with a cross-reference to section 2416 and the statement *"and except as otherwise provided by Congress."* It also contains a variety of additional exceptions to the general six year period in subsections (b)-(i) of section 2415. To put it bluntly, section 2415 is a perfect example of how not to draft a statute.

b.   Punctuate With Care

There are many advantages to electronic communications such as email, texting, and tweeting, but they have wreaked more havoc on the proper use of punctuation marks than even the decline in the teaching of grammar in the 1960s and 70s. Fortunately, there has been a revival of interest in proper punctuation, highlighted by the popularity of Lynn Truss' book *Eats, Shoots and Leaves.*

Whatever may be the value of punctuation in the rest of the world of the written word, in the drafting of statutes and rules, proper punctuation it is of crucial

---

[15] G. Coode, Legislative Expression 50-53 (1845).

importance. The common wisdom is that English statutes were originally written without punctuation, citing Bentham and others. Mellinkofff calls this criticism a canard and says the English Parliament always used punctuation.[16] Whatever the accuracy of the traditional criticism, the fact today is that courts rely heavily on punctuation in interpreting a statute or rule. It thus becomes just as important for the statute or rule drafter to be as careful in the use of punctuation marks as in word choice or sentence structure.

A full treatment of punctuation is no more appropriate for this book than a full treatment of grammar. There are, however, several key rules of punctuation that are particularly important in drafting a statute or rule to avoid a possible misinterpretation by a court or other reader.

1.   Colon:

    a.   use only to introduce a tabulation;

    b.   do not use to introduce a proviso (even more important, do not use a proviso, see sec. [a] above).

2.   Semicolon:

    a.   use only in a tabulation of clauses to separate the clauses tabulated;

    b.   do not use as a substitute for a period to separate independent clauses.

3.   Comma:

    a.   Put a comma before "*and*" or "*or*" when the last two items in a series or list are separate items (*a taxpayer shall list earned income, interest, capital gains, and royalties*) to make it clear that capital gains and royalties are not to be combined as a single item. It has become common for writers and even grammarians to challenge the need for the comma at this location, but the need for clarity in a statute or rule demands it.

    b.   Use a period rather than a comma to separate the clauses of a compound sentence that are joined by an "*and*." The sentence "*An appellant shall file a brief within 60 days of the filing of the record and shall include in the brief a statement of facts . . .*" should read "*An appellant shall file a brief within 60 days of filing of the record. The appellant shall include in the brief a statement of facts . . .*"

    c.   Use a comma to show that qualifying words that follow several words or clauses apply to all of the preceding words or clauses (*An applicant shall submit a resume showing education, relevant work experience, and compensation history for the previous five years*). Here, if there is not a comma after *relevant work experience* it is unclear whether the qualifier *for the previous five years* applies only to compensation history or to relevant work experience, or even to education. Another way to show which of the three items the five year limitation applies to is to put it

---

[16]   D. Mellinkoff, The Language of the Law 157 (1963).

before all of those to which it applies (*An applicant shall submit a resume showing education, relevant work experience, and for the past five years compensation history*). Some might put commas both before and after *for the past five years* but that would not add to clarity and would make the clause more difficult to read.

c. Tabulate for Clarity

There are few structural devices the drafter can use to bring clarity to a statute or rule more useful than to tabulate a recital of three or more of anything — nouns, verbs, objects, complements, exceptions, qualifiers, or limitations.

Tabulation has two principal benefits. The first is the obvious one — it helps the reader understand the sentence or section. The second, and just as important, it helps both the drafter and the proponent identify the various options available to expand or narrow the effect of the statute or rule being drafted.

The first major proponent of tabulation as an aid to clarity in both analysis and readability was Dickerson, first in his book *Legislative Drafting* and then in *The Fundamentals of Legal Drafting.*

A basic rule for tabulating is that the words must be of the same class so that the sentence would read properly if only one of the words were included in the sentence.

A simple example of tabulation is 28 U.S.C. § 2284(b)(3) quoted and revised in section [3][a], above. The last sentence of the revised section provides that *"The single judge may not appoint a master, order a reference, hear or grant an application for or to vacate a preliminary injunction, or enter a judgment on the merits."* Tabulating the list of actions the single judge may not do would read:

The single judge may not:

i. appoint a master;

ii. order a reference;

iii. hear or grant an application for or to vacate a preliminary or permanent injunction; or

iv. enter a judgement on the merits.

Another more complicated example is 28 U.S.C. § 2509, dealing with referral by a House of Congress of a claim against the United States. Subsection (g) provides:

The Court of Federal Claims is hereby authorized and directed, under such regulations as it may prescribe, to provide the facilities and services of the office of the clerk of the court for the filing, processing, hearing, and dispatch of congressional reference cases and to include within its annual appropriations the costs thereof and other costs of administration, including (but without limitation to the items herein listed) the salaries and traveling expenses of the judges serving as hearing officers and panel members, mailing and service of process, necessary physical facilities, equipment, and supplies, and personnel (including secretaries and law clerks).

Without totally rewriting the section, as should be done, and limiting the rewrite to the listing of the items the Court should include in its budget, the listing should read:

> *the costs of determining congressional reference cases including:*
>
> i.　*salaries and travelling expenses of judges serving as hearing officers or panel members;*
>
> ii.　*mailing and service of process;*
>
> iii.　*necessary physical facilities;*
>
> iv.　*equipment;*
>
> v.　*supplies; and*
>
> vi.　*personnel, including secretaries and law clerks.*

In a tabulation it is important for the drafter to use an *"and"* or *"or"* after the penultimate item listed and to determine which is appropriate. If the tabulation is cumulative and all are to be included, use *"and."* If, on the other hand, the list is in the alternative and only one is applicable, then *"or"* should be used. If one or more of the items can be applicable, then the list should have the introductory phrase *"one or more of the following."*

Chapter 13

RULES ON DRAFTING SPECIFIC PROVISIONS OR WORDS

A. INTRODUCTION

In addition to the general principles and rules set out in Chapter 12 on drafting the simple declarative sentences that constitute the heart of a statute or rule, there are special types of provisions or words that call for specific rules to achieve brevity, simplicity, clarity, and consistency, all hallmarks of good drafting. These rules are not a direct product of Plain English but are complementary to it.

B. DEFINITIONS

1. When to Define

Whether a drafter should define a word in a statute or rule depends on a number of factors: the number of times the word is used, its importance to the substance of the statute or rule, possible inconsistency in its use, and whether it has an accepted meaning that will prevent those affected by it or the courts from giving it different interpretations. The more important it is to the statute or rule's proponent to control the interpretation of a word in it, the more important it is for the drafter to define the word.

If a word is used only once, then its definition rather than the word itself should be included in the sentence. Thus the drafter should use *person age 18 or over* if the phrase is used only once. If more than once, the drafter should use *adult* with the definition *adult means a person age 18 or over.*

2. Placement of Definition

If it is necessary to define a word, the drafter should place it at the beginning of the lowest subdivision of the statute or rule in which it is used. If it is used throughout the entire statute or rule that includes several chapters, then there should be a separate chapter for definitions. The same applies for each lower subdivision of the statute or rule, i.e., section, subsection, paragraph, or subparagraph.

A separate subdivision entitled *Definitions* should be used only if the subdivision includes definitions of more than one word. If there is only one definition, then the subdivision should begin with the words *In this (title, chapter, section) "adult" means a person age 18 or over.*

3.   The Difference Between *"Means"* and *"Includes"*

A definition can be one of two types — exhaustive or partial. Exhaustive means that it includes all possibilities. If something falls outside the definition, it is not included (*natural person means a human being*). A definition is partial if it can include something not listed (*school includes an elementary or secondary institution*). It has been traditional for a partial definition to read *includes but is not limited to*. Nothing but *includes* is necessary. The additional words add only additional words but no additional meaning. The drafter should not use them. If they are in one definition but not another, a court will try to figure out a reason for the difference and may conclude one is exhaustive and the other partial when both are intended to be partial.

4.   Do Not Include Substantive Provisions With the Definition

A bad habit of some drafters is to include a substantive provision in the sentence with the definition (*The record includes all pleadings, documents, exhibits, and transcripts of testimony which the clerk shall forward to the court of appeals within 30 days of the filing of the notice of appeal*). This sentence should be broken into two sentences, one that defines *record* and the other that imposes the forwarding duty on the clerk. (The items in the list should, of course, be in the singular, not plural).

5.   Exclude the Word Defined from the Definition

Another bad habit of some drafters is to include the word defined in the definition (*a medical facility is a facility in which medical services are provided*). This type of definition serves no purpose because it does not add anything to the word or words being defined. More helpful would be (*a medical facility means a building, vehicle, or other physical area in which a medical service is provided*).

6.   Include Only Words That are Commonly Understood to Fit Within the Word Defined

Another trap the drafter can fall into is to think that the definition can include anything, even things that most people would not think would be included, especially words that usually mean the opposite. Thus *yes* should not be defined to mean *an affirmative or negative response* or *boat* to include *automobile* or *house*, *apple* to include *orange*, or *roadway* to include *waterway*. This type of abuse of the legislative power is simply a trap for the unwary that the careful drafter should always avoid.

C.   CONDITIONS AND EXCEPTIONS

1.   Conditions — *If, When,* or *Where*

Some drafters of statutes and rules often misuse *if, when*, and *where*. The correct usage is as follows:

a. *If*

A drafter should use *if* only to state a condition precedent, that is, a prerequisite to bringing the provision into play (*If a voter does not have the required identification, the voter may cast only a provisional ballot*). Do not use *when* or *where* in this type of provision. As in the example, the proper placement of the condition is at the beginning of the sentence. If there are several conditions, the drafter should state the rule first, and then list the conditions (*A voter may vote only in the precinct of the voter's residence. If a voter attempts to vote in another precinct or has no proof of residence, the voter may not vote*). If the number of conditions is more than two, tabulation may be appropriate.

b. *When*

The drafter should use *when* only when there is a time sequence between an event that the provision presumes will happen and a later event that automatically follows the first event (*When a student completes the required courses, the school shall award the student a degree*). The drafter should also not use *whenever* rather than *when*. The extra *ever* adds nothing except length.

c. *Where*

A common mistake in all writing including the drafting of a statute or rule is to use *where* instead of *if* or *when*. The correct usage is only when (not *where*) the provision applies to a physical place (*An applicant shall include the address where the applicant resides*).

2. Exceptions

There are two techniques for a drafter to exclude a person, action, place, circumstance, or event from the operation of a statute or rule. One is to make the exception by starting a provision with the word *except* (*Except for a person under age 18, a requirement applies to a resident of the city; Except as otherwise provided in the previous section, a resident shall*). This format is appropriate if the recital of the exception is short. If the exception is longer, it is usually better to put in in a separate subsequent sentence (*This requirement does not apply to a resident age 65 or older, a non-resident, or a short term renter*).

3. Establishment of a Governmental Entity or Position

There are two commonly used techniques to establish a governmental entity or office. The first is to do so expressly (*There is hereby created the Department of Public Safety. The Secretary of the Department shall administer it*) with subsequent provisions establishing duties and powers of the Department or of the Secretary.

Another is to create the entity or office indirectly by simply providing for the powers and duties of the entity or office (*The Department of Public Safety shall enforce a law making an act a crime; The Secretary of the Department of Public Safety is the head of the Department and shall supervise its employees*).

While the second technique is shorter because it takes only one provision to both create the entity or office and to provide for its powers and duties, the drafter of the statute or rule should follow the common practice in the jurisdiction for similar entities and offices.

4. Penalty

There are substantial inconsistencies in the manner in which a statute or rule imposes a penalty. The simplest and best way is to provide for the penalty (*The penalty for violating this section is*). All of the other ways are more convoluted such as providing that *A person who violates the section is subject to a penalty of.* There is no need for the longer provision when the shorter will do the same thing.

If there are more than two penalties provided, tabulation may be advisable. In tabulating the penalties, it is important to distinguish between penalties that are cumulative and those that are only alternatives. Under the tabulating rules, if the penalties are cumulative, *and* is used before the last item in the tabulation. If they are in the alternative, *or* is used. Needless to say the distinction is important.

If the jurisdiction for which the drafter is preparing a penalty provision uses a classification system for its crimes with prescribed penalties for each class, then it is necessary for the drafter only to classify the crime to establish the desired penalty. It is, of course, up to the proponent of the provision to determine the level of punishment. The task of the drafter is to make the proponent aware of the options and follow the choice made by the proponent.

5. Age, Day, Date, Number, and Time

a. Age

When a drafter seeks to put an age in a statute or rule, the correct way to do it will depend upon whether the intent is to include persons over or under a certain age, or both. When under, say *under age 21*. If older, say *age 21 or older.* To set a minimum and maximum age, say *age 21 or older but under age 65.* Do not add the words *of age.* They are superfluous. No one will think the intent is to refer to weight.

b. Day and Date

For some reason, it has become common to use *July Fourth* or *July the Fourth* to refer to the particular day of a month. This is incorrect. *Fourth* is an ordinal number (see section [c], below), an adjective, and is actually a contraction for *the Fourth day of July.* Correct usage is *July 4.* (*July Four* is also correct but is longer and not as easy to read.)

If the reference is to a particular date rather than to a particular day, it should read *July 4, 1776, or after*, with a comma both before and after the year. If the reference is only to a month and a year, the reference should have a comma only after the year (*July 1776, or after*).

c.   Number

A drafter can use three types of numbers in a statute or rule. The first is a cardinal or Arabic number (*1, 10, 100*). The second is an ordinal (*tenth* or *10th, twenty first* or *21st*), which is an adjective and needs a noun to be complete (*tenth person, twenty first birthday*). The third is a fraction which can be expressed in words (*one sixteenth*) or numbers (*1/16th*). It also is an adjective which needs a noun to be complete (*1/6th of a section*).

Express a cardinal number in an Arabic numeral rather than a word (*The appellant shall file its brief within 30 days*). When, however, the number is the first word in a sentence, spell it out (*Twenty days after the appellant files its brief*). Both ordinal and fractional numbers, being adjectives, are written in words, not numerals (*the twentieth day, a quarter pound*).

6.   Capital Letters

It is common in statutes and rules as well as in general writing to capitalize many more words than necessary. The best and simplest rule to follow is to capitalize only the first word of a sentence and proper nouns. It is rare for a proper noun to be in a statute or rule except when referring to an entity or officer of government (*department of state, treasurer*). There is no reason to capitalize either except when a government official's proper name is used (*President Lincoln*).

7.   Hyphen

A hyphen is used to join together two separate words to express a single thought. It is traditional when the two words are first used together to keep them separate. As the usage becomes more common the writer uses a hyphen. Even later, the hyphen is dropped and the two words become one. The most common example today is *email.* It started out as *electronic mail*, then became *e-mail*, and is swiftly becoming *email.*

In view of the fact that language, and particularly compounding of words, is always in a state of transition from two words to one and statutes and rules have an indefinite length, the wise drafter will prefer the final single word over the temporary hyphenated word. If the combined word looks awkward or forced, use two words, but not the hyphenated word (*super majority, supermajority*).

8.   Cross Reference

It is sometimes necessary and often convenient for the drafter to refer to a prior or subsequent provision in the statute or rule being drafted or to a separate statute or rule. A cross reference creates a problem for the reader of the statute or rule, because an understanding of the new statute or rule requires looking up the cross reference. This may not be a major problem if the cross reference is to the same statute or rule or to a statute or rule of the same law making body for which the draft is being prepared and that body's enactments or adoptions are published in an easily accessible source. Today, publication and accessibility are much less of a problem, because most of these items are available on the internet. Previously, access was limited to books or files that may not have been widely available.

Notwithstanding easier access to other statutes and rules, the drafter should use a cross reference only when necessary. When used, a cross reference within the statute or rule being drafted should not be to a location relative to the provision being drafted (*the preceding subsection, as provided above*) but to the section, subsection, or paragraph being referenced (*section 2, subsection 2 A, paragraph 2 A (1)*). Do not spell out the subdivision except for the first word. Thus, for subsection 2(A)(1), do not say *section 2, subsection A, paragraph (1)*.

A common problem with a cross reference is whether the cross reference is to the provision as it exists at the time of the enactment of the new statute or adoption of the new rule is intended to include any subsequent amendments to the provision. Unless there is a provision to the contrary, the general rule is that the cross reference is to the statute or rule as it was at the time of the enactment or adoption of the cross reference. If the intent is to include any later amendments, the drafter should include a clause saying so (*including any amendment enacted (adopted) after the effective date of this Act (rule)*).

Appendix

EXAMPLES OF BILLS AND ORDINANCE

I

112TH CONGRESS
1ST SESSION

H. R. 39

To delist the polar bear as a threatened species under the Endangered
Species Act of 1973.

IN THE HOUSE OF REPRESENTATIVES

JANUARY 5, 2011

Mr. YOUNG of Alaska introduced the following bill; which was referred to the
Committee on Natural Resources

A BILL

To delist the polar bear as a threatened species under the
Endangered Species Act of 1973.

1   *Be it enacted by the Senate and House of Representa-*

2 *tives of the United States of America in Congress assembled,*

3 **SECTION 1. SHORT TITLE.**

4   This Act may be cited as the "Polar Bear Delisting

5 Act".

6 **SEC. 2. DELISTING OF POLAR BEAR AS THREATENED SPE-**

7   **CIES.**

8   The determination by the United States Fish and

9 Wildlife of the threatened status for the polar bear (Ursus

10 maritimus) under the Endangered Species Act of 1973

2

1 (16 U.S.C. 1531 et seq.), published May 15, 2008 (73

2 Fed. Reg. 28211 et seq.), and the listing of such species

3 as a threatened species under that Act pursuant to such

4 determination, shall have no force or effect.

○

State of Wisconsin
2011 - 2012 LEGISLATURE
January 2011 Special Session

 CORRECTED COPY

LRB-0832/2
MES:jld&wlj:md

ASSEMBLY BILL 2

January 4, 2011 - Introduced by COMMITTEE ON ASSEMBLY ORGANIZATION, by request of Governor Scott Walker, Representative Kaufert, and Senator Darling. Referred to Committee on Health.

1   AN ACT *to create* 71.07 (6f) and 71.10 (4) (cf) of the statutes; **relating to:** creating

2   a nonrefundable individual income tax credit for certain amounts relating to

3   health savings accounts that may be deducted from, or are exempt from, federal

4   income taxes.

Analysis by the Legislative Reference Bureau

Under current federal law, certain individuals may make tax–deductible contributions to health savings accounts (HSAs) and withdraw the money tax–free when needed to cover routine and preventive medical care.

Under this bill, an individual who makes contributions to such an HSA may claim a nonrefundable income tax credit for 6.5 percent of the allowable amount that the individual claims as a federal tax deduction for a contribution to an HSA or 6.5 percent of the federal tax–exempt earnings relating to an HSA, or both.

For further information see the *state* fiscal estimate, which will be printed as an appendix to this bill.

The people of the state of Wisconsin, represented in senate and assembly, do enact as follows:

5   SECTION 1. 71.07 (6f) of the statutes is created to read:

1   71.07 **(6f)** HEALTH SAVINGS ACCOUNT TAX CREDIT. (a) *Definitions.* In this

2   subsection:

3   1. "Claimant" means an individual who claims a deduction for a contribution

4   to, or who claims federal tax–exempt earnings relating to, a health savings account

5   under section 223 of the Internal Revenue Code.

6   2. "Deduction amount" means the allowable amount of a deduction claimed on

7   a claimant's federal income tax return for a contribution to a health savings account

8   under section 223 of the Internal Revenue Code, or federal tax–exempt earnings

9   relating to a health savings account under section 223 of the Internal Revenue Code.

10   (b) *Filing claims.* Subject to the limitations provided in this subsection, a

11   claimant may claim as a credit against the tax imposed under s. 71.02, up to the

12   amount of those taxes, 6.5 percent of the deduction amount claimed in the taxable

13   year to which the claim under this subsection relates.

14   (c) *Limitations.* 1. No credit may be allowed under this subsection unless it

15   is claimed within the time period under s. 71.75 (2).

16   2. For a claimant who is a nonresident or part–year resident of this state and

17   who is a single person or a married person filing a separate return, multiply the

18   credit for which the claimant is eligible under par. (b) by a fraction the numerator of

19   which is the individual's Wisconsin adjusted gross income and the denominator of

20   which is the individual's federal adjusted gross income. If a claimant is married and

21   files a joint return, and if the claimant or the claimant's spouse, or both, are

22   nonresidents or part–year residents of this state, multiply the credit for which the

23   claimant is eligible under par. (b) by a fraction the numerator of which is the couple's

24   joint Wisconsin adjusted gross income and the denominator of which is the couple's

25   joint federal adjusted gross income.

1   (d) *Administration.* Subsection (9e) (d), to the extent that it applies to the credit

2 under that subsection, applies to the credit under this subsection.

3   SECTION 2. 71.10 (4) (cf) of the statutes is created to read:

4   71.10 **(4)** (cf) The health savings account tax credit under s. 71.07 (6f).

5   **SECTION 3. Nonstatutory provisions.**

6   (1) REQUIRED GENERAL FUND BALANCE. Section 20.003 (4) of the statutes does not

7 apply to the action of the legislature in enacting this act.

8   **SECTION 4. Initial applicability.**

9   (1) This act first applies to taxable years beginning on January 1 of the year

10 in which this subsection takes effect, except that if this subsection takes effect after

11 July 31 this act first applies to taxable years beginning on January 1 of the year

12 following the year in which this subsection takes effect.

13   **(END)**

Model Municipal Noise Ordinance

ARTICLE 1: PURPOSE

1.1. WHEREAS excessive sound is a serious hazard to the public health, welfare, safety, and the quality of life; and, WHEREAS a substantial body of science and technology exists by which excessive sound may be substantially abated; and, WHEREAS the people have a right to, and should be ensured an environment free from excessive sound, it is the policy of _____ to prevent excessive sound that may jeopardize the health, welfare, or safety of the citizens or degrade the quality of life.

1.2. This ordinance shall apply to the control of sound originating from stationary sources within the limits of _____

ARTICLE 2: DEFINITIONS

The following words and terms, when used in this ordinance, shall have the following meanings unless the context clearly indicates otherwise.

2.1. "Ambient Sound Level" is the total sound pressure level in the area of interest including the noise source of interest.

2.2. "A-Weighting" is the electronic filtering in sound level meters that models human hearing frequency sensitivity.

2.3. "Background Sound Level" is the total sound pressure level in the area of interest excluding the noise source of interest.

2.4. "Commercial Area" is a group of commercial facilities and the abutting public right-of-way and public spaces.

2.5. "Commercial Facility" is any premises, property, or facility involving traffic in goods or furnishing of services for sale or profit, including but not limited to:
   a.   Banking and other financial institutions;
   b.   Dining establishments;
   c.   Establishments for providing retail or wholesale services;
   d.   Establishments for recreation and entertainment;
   e.   Office buildings;
   f.   Transportation; and
   g.   Warehouses.

2.6. "Construction" is any site preparation, assembly, erection, repair, alteration or similar action, or demolition of buildings or structures.

2.7. "C-Weighting" is the electronic filtering in sound level meters that models a flat response (output equals input) over the range of maximum human hearing frequency sensitivity.

2.8. "dBA" is the A-weighted unit of sound pressure level.

2.9. "dBC" is the C-weighted unit of sound pressure level.

2.10. "Decibel (dB)" is the unit of measurement for sound pressure level at a specified location.

2.11. "Emergency Work" is any work or action necessary to deliver essential services including, but not limited to, repairing water, gas, electric, telephone, sewer facilities, or public transportation facilities, removing fallen trees on public rights-of-way, or abating life-threatening conditions.

2.12. "Impulsive Sound" is a sound having a duration of less that 1 s with an abrupt onset and rapid decay.

2.13. "Industrial Facility" is any activity and its related premises, property, facilities, or equipment involving the fabrication, manufacture, or production of durable or nondurable goods.

2.14. "Motor Vehicle" is any vehicle that is propelled or drawn on land by an engine or motor.

2.15. "Muffler" is a sound-dissipative device or system for attenuating the sound of escaping gases of an internal combustion engine.

2.16. "Multi-dwelling Unit Building" is any building wherein there are two or more dwelling units.

2.17. "The Municipality" is (*name of municipality in question.*)

2.18. "Noise" is any sound of such level and duration as to be or tend to be injurious to human health or welfare, or which would unreasonably interfere with the enjoyment of life or property throughout the

Municipality or in any portions thereof, but excludes all aspects of the employer-employee relationship concerning health and safety hazards within the confines of a place of employment.

2.19. "Noise Control Administrator (NCA)" is the noise control officer designated as the official liaison with all municipal departments, empowered to grant permits for variances.

2.20. "Noise Control Officer (NCO)" is an officially designated employee of the Municipality trained in the measurement of sound and empowered to issue a summons for violations of this ordinance.

2.21. "Noise Disturbance" is any sound that (a) endangers the safety or health of any person, (b) disturbs a reasonable person of normal sensitivities, or (c) endangers personal or real property.

2.22. "Person" is any individual, corporation, company, association, society, firm partnership, joint stock company, the Municipality or any political subdivision, agency or instrumentality of the Municipality.

2.23. "Public right-of-way" is any street, avenue, boulevard, road, highway, sidewalk, or alley that is leased, owned, or controlled by a governmental entity.

2.24. "Public Space" is any real property or structures thereon that is owned, leased, or controlled by a governmental entity.

2.25. "Pure Tone" is any sound that can be judged as a single pitch or set of single pitches by the NCO.

2.26. "Real Property Line" is either (a) the imaginary line, including its vertical extension, that separates one parcel of real property from another, or (b) the vertical and horizontal boundaries of a dwelling unit that is one in a multi-dwelling unit building.

2.27. "Residential Area" is a group of residential properties and the abutting public rights-of-way and public spaces.

2.28. "Residential Property" is property used for human habitation, including but not limited to:
   a. Private property used for human habitation;
   b. Commercial living accommodations and commercial property used for human habitation;
   c. Recreational and entertainment property used for human habitation; and
   d. Community service property used for human habitation.

2.29. "Sound Level" is the instantaneous sound pressure level measured in decibels with a sound level meter set for A-weighting on slow integration speed, unless otherwise noted.

2.30. "Measuring Instrument" is an instrument such as a sound level meter, integrating sound level meter or dosimeter used to measure sound pressure levels conforming to Type 1 or Type 2 standards as specified in the latest version of ANSI Standard S1.4-1983.

2.31. "Sound Pressure Level (SPL)" is 20 multiplied by the logarithm, to the base 10, of the measured sound pressure divided by the sound pressure associated with the threshold of human hearing, in units of decibels.

2.32. "Weekday" is any day, Monday through Friday, that is not a legal holiday.

ARTICLE 3: POWERS, DUTIES AND QUALIFICATIONS OF THE NOISE CONTROL OFFICERS AND ADMINISTRATORS

3.1. The provisions of this ordinance shall be enforced by the noise control officers (NCOs).

3.2. The noise control administrator (NCA) shall have the power to:
   a. Coordinate the noise control activities of all municipal departments and cooperate with all other public bodies and agencies to the extent practicable;
   b. Review the actions of other municipal departments and advise such departments to the effect, if any, of such actions on noise control;
   c. Review public and private projects, subject to mandatory review or approval by other departments or boards, for compliance with this ordinance; and
   d. Grant permits for variances according to the provisions of Article 9.

3.3. A person shall be qualified to be an NCO if the person has satisfactorily completed any of the following:
   a. An instructional program in community noise from a certified noise control engineer, as evidenced by certification from the Institute of Noise Control Engineering (INCE);
   b. An instructional program in community noise from another NCO; or
   c. Education or experience or a combination thereof certified by the NCA as equivalent to the provisions of (a) or (b) of this section.

3.4. Noise measurements taken by a NCO shall be taken in accordance with the procedures specified in Article 5.

ARTICLE 4: DUTIES AND RESPONSIBILITIES OF OTHER DEPARTMENTS

4.1. All departments and agencies of the Municipality shall carry out their programs according to law and shall cooperate with the NCA in the implementation and enforcement of this ordinance.

4.2. All departments charged with new projects or changes to existing projects that may result in the production of noise shall consult with the NCA prior to the approval of such projects to ensure that such activities comply with the provisions of this ordinance.

ARTICLE 5: SOUND MEASUREMENT PROCEDURES

5.1. Insofar as practicable, sound will be measured while the source under investigation is operating at normal, routine conditions and, as necessary, at other conditions, including but not limited to, design, maximum, and fluctuating rates.

5.2. All tests shall be conducted in accordance with the following procedures:

   a. The NCO shall, to the extent practicable, identify all sources contributing sound to the point of measurement.

   b. Measurements shall be taken at or within the property line of the affected person.

   c. The measuring instrument must be calibrated using a calibrator recommended by the measuring instrument manufacturer before and after each series of readings.

   d. The measuring instrument must be recertified and the calibrator must be recalibrated at least once each year by the manufacturer or by a person that has been approved by the manufacturer. A copy of written documentation of such recertification and recalibration shall be kept with the equipment to which it refers.

   e. No outdoor measurements shall be taken:

      1. During periods when wind speeds (including gusts) exceed 15 mph;

      2. Without a windscreen, recommended by the measuring instrument manufacturer, properly attached to the measuring instrument;

      3. Under any condition that allows the measuring instrument to become wet (e.g., rain, snow, or condensation);or

      4. When the ambient temperature is out of the range of the tolerance of the measuring instrument.

5.3. The report for each measurement session shall include:

   a. The date, day of the week, and times at which measurements are taken;

   b. The times of calibration;

   c. The weather conditions;

   d. The identification of all monitoring equipment by manufacturer, model number, and serial number;

   e. The normal operating cycle of the sources in question with a description of the sources;

   f. The ambient sound level, in dBA, with the sources in question operating;

   g. The background sound level, in dBA, without the sources in question operating; and

   h. A sketch of the measurement site, including measurement locations and relevant distances, containing sufficient information for another investigator to repeat the measurements under similar conditions.

5.4. Prior to taking noise measurements the investigator shall explore the vicinity of the source in question to identify any other sound sources that could affect measurements, to establish the approximate location and character of the principal sound source, and to select suitable locations from which to measure the sound from the source in question.

5.5. When measuring continuous sound, or sound that is sustained for more that 1 s at a time, the measuring instrument shall be set for A-weighting, slow response, and the range (if the measuring instrument is designed to read levels over different ranges) shall be set to that range in which the meter reads closest to the middle of the scale. The minimum and maximum readings shall be recorded to indicate the range of monitored values along with the central tendency average most often displayed.

5.6. The measuring instrument shall be placed at a minimum height of 3 ft above the ground or from any reflective surface. When handheld, the microphone shall be held at arm's length and pointed at the source at the angle recommended by the measuring instruments manufacturer.

5.7. If extraneous sound sources, such as aircraft flyovers or barking dogs, that are unrelated to the measurements increase the monitored sound levels, the measurements should be postponed until these extraneous sounds have become of such a level as not to increase the monitored sound levels of interest.

5.8. The monitoring session should last for a period of time sufficient to ensure that the sound levels measured are typical of the source in question.

5.9. The background sound levels shall be subtracted from the measured sound levels of the source of interest by using Table 1 to determine the sound levels from the source of interest alone. If the ambient sound level is less than 3 dBA higher than the background sound level, the source level cannot be derived and a violation of the ordinance cannot be substantiated.

Table 1 Correction for Background Levels*

Difference Between Ambient and Background Sound Levels	Correction Factor to Be Subtracted from Ambient Level for Source Level
3	3
4,5	2
6-9	1
10 or more	0

*In dBA

ARTICLE 6: SOUND LEVEL LIMITATIONS

6.1. No person shall cause, suffer, allow, or permit the operation of any sound source on a particular category of property or any public space or right-of-way in such a manner as to create a sound level that exceeds the background sound level by at least 10 dBA during daytime (7:00 a.m. to 10:00 p.m.) hours and by at least 5 dBA during nighttime (10:00 p.m. to 7:00 a.m.) hours when measured at or within the real property line of the receiving property, except as provided in Section 6.1.1. Such a sound source would constitute a noise disturbance.

    6.1.1. If the background sound level cannot be determined, the absolute sound level limits set forth in Table 2 shall be used.

    6.1.2. If the sound source in question is a pure tone, the limits of Table 2 shall be reduced by 5 dBA.

TABLE 2 Maximum Permissible Sound Levels*   Receiving Property

	Residential		Commercial
Source Property	7:00 a.m.-10:00 p.m.	10:00 p.m.-7:00 a.m.	(All times)
Residential	55	50	65
Commercial	65	50	65
Industrial	65	50	65

*In dBA. These levels would be appropriate for typical suburban environments. Urban environments may allow for limits that are 5 to 10 dBA higher and rural or quiet suburban environments may allow for limits that are 5 to 10 dBA lower than those listed. The specific limitations should be based on the environment and tastes of the municipality.

    6.1.3. Nonrepetitive impulsive sound sources shall not exceed 90 dBA or 120 dBA at or within a residential real property line, using the fast meter response speed.

    6.1.4. In multi-dwelling unit buildings, if the background sound level cannot be determined, the daytime limit is 45 dBA and the nighttime limit is 35 dBA for sounds originating in another dwelling within the same building.

6.2. The following are exempt from the sound level limits of Section 6.1:

    a. Noise from emergency signaling devices;

98-517
Rev. A

    b.   Noise from an exterior burglar alarm of any building provided such burglar alarm shall terminate its operation within 5 min of its activation;

    c.   Noise from domestic power tools, lawn mowers, and agricultural equipment when operated between 7:00 a.m. and 8:00 p.m. on weekdays and between 8:00 a.m. and 8:00 p.m. on weekends and legal holidays, provided they generate less than 85 dBA at or within any real property line of a residential property;

    d.   Sound from church bells and chimes when a part of a religious observance or service;

    e.   Noise from construction activity provided all motorized equipment used in such activity is equipped with functioning mufflers, except as provided in Section 7.2(f);

    f.   Noise from snow blowers, snow throwers, and snow plows when operated with a muffler for the purpose of snow removal.

6.3   When the source being analyzed is a stereo system with low frequency signals as part of its output, the stereo shall not cause a "C" weighted level of 10dB or greater above the "C" weighted ambient level at a distance of 10 feet from the source, or the complainant's property line, which ever is greater.

ARTICLE 7: SPECIFIC PROHIBITED ACTS

7.1.   No person shall cause, suffer, allow, or permit to be made verbally or mechanically any noise disturbance, as defined in Section 6.1.

7.2.   No person shall cause, suffer, allow, or permit the following acts:

    a.   Operating, playing, or permitting the operation or playing of any radio, television, phonograph, or similar device that reproduces or amplifies sound in such a manner as to create a noise disturbance (as defined in Section 6.1) for any person other than the operator of the device;

    b.   Using or operating any loudspeaker, public address system, or similar device between 10:00 p.m. and 8:00 a.m. the following day, such that the sound therefrom creates a noise disturbance (as defined in Section 6.1) across a residential real property line;

    c.   Owning, possessing, or harboring any animal or bird that, frequently or for continued duration, generates sounds that create a noise disturbance (as defined in Section 6.1) across a residential real property line;

    d.   Loading, unloading, opening, closing, or other handling of boxes, crates, containers, building materials, liquids, garbage cans, refuse, or similar objects, or the pneumatic or pumped loading or unloading of bulk materials in liquid, gaseous, powder, or pellet form, or the compacting of refuse by persons engaged in the business of scavenging or garbage collection, whether private or municipal, between 9:00 p.m. and 7:00 a.m. the following day on a weekday and between 9:00 p.m. and 9:00 a.m. the following day on a weekend day or legal holiday except by permit, when the sound therefrom creates a noise disturbance (as defined in Section 6.1) across a residential property line;

    e.   Operating or permitting the operation of any motor vehicle whose manufacturer's gross weight rating is in excess of 10,000 lbs, or any auxiliary equipment attached to such a vehicle, for a period of longer than 5 min in any hour while the vehicle is stationary, for reasons other than traffic congestion or emergency work, on a public right-of-way or public space within 150 ft of a residential area between 8:00 p.m. and 8:00 a.m. the following day;

    f.   Operating or permitting the operation of any tools or equipment used in construction, drilling, earthmoving, excavating, or demolition work between 6:00 p.m. and 7:00 a.m. the following day on a weekday or at any time on a weekend day or legal holiday, except for emergency work, by variance issued pursuant to Article 9, or when the sound level does not exceed any applicable relative or absolute limit specified in Section 6.1.

ARTICLE 8: EXEMPTIONS

8.1.   The provisions of this ordinance shall not apply to:

    a.   The generation of sound for the purpose of alerting persons to the existence of an emergency except as provided in Section 6.2(b);

    b.   The generation of sound in the performance of emergency work; or

    c.   The generation of sound in situations within the jurisdiction of the Federal Occupational Safety and Health Administration.

8.2. Noise generated from municipally sponsored or approved celebrations or events shall be exempt from the provisions of this ordinance.

ARTICLE 9: VARIANCE CONDITIONS

9.1. Any person who owns or operates any stationary noise source may apply to the NCA for a variance from one or more of the provisions of this ordinance. Applications for a permit of variance shall supply information including, but not limited to:

    a.   The nature and location of the noise source for which such application is made;

    b.   The reason for which the permit of variance is requested, including the hardship that will result to the applicant, his/her client, or the public if the permit of variance is not granted;

    c.   The level of noise that will occur during the period of the variance;

    d.   The section or sections of this ordinance for which the permit of variance shall apply;

    e.   A description of interim noise control measures to be taken for the applicant to minimize noise and the impacts occurring therefrom; and

    f.   A specific schedule of the noise control measures that shall be taken to bring the source into compliance with this ordinance within a reasonable time.

       9.1.1. Failure to supply the information required by the NCA shall be cause for rejection of the application.

       9.1.2. A copy of the permit of variance must be kept on file by the municipal clerk for public inspection.

9.2. The NCA may charge the applicant a fee of $_____ to cover expenses resulting from the processing of the permit of variance application.

9.3. The NCA may, at his/her discretion, limit the duration of the permit of variance, which shall be no longer than 1 year. Any person holding a permit of variance and requesting an extension of time shall apply for a new permit of variance under the provisions of this section.

9.4. No variance shall be approved unless the applicant presents adequate proof that:

    a.   Noise levels occurring during the period of the variance will not constitute a danger to public health; and

    b.   Compliance with the ordinance would impose an unreasonable hardship on the applicant without equal or greater benefits to the public.

9.5. In making the determination of granting a variance, the NCA shall consider:

    a.   the character and degree of injury to, or interference with, the health and welfare or the reasonable use of property that is caused or threatened to be caused;

    b.   The social and economic value of the activity for which the variance is sought; and

    c.   The ability of the applicant to apply the best practical noise control measures.

9.6. The permit of variance may be revoked by the NCA if the terms of the permit of variance are violated.

9.7. A variance may be revoked by the NCA if there is:

    a.   Violation of one or more conditions of the variance;

    b.   Material misrepresentation of fact in the variance application; or

    c.   Material change in any of the circumstances relied on by the NCA in granting the variance.

ARTICLE 10: ENFORCEMENT PROCEDURES

10.1. Violation of any provision of this ordinance shall be cause for a summons to be issued by the NCO according to procedures set forth in (*Administrative Code reference*).

10.2. In lieu of issuing a summons as provided in Section 10.1, the NCO may issue an order requiring abatement of any sound source alleged to be in violation of this ordinance within a reasonable time period and according to guidelines that the NCO may prescribe.

10.3. Any person who violates any provision of this ordinance shall be subject to a fine for each offense of not more than $_____.

       10.3.1. If the violation is of a continuing nature, each day during which it occurs shall constitute an additional, separate, and distinct offense.

10.4. No provision of this ordinance shall be construed to impair any common law or statutory cause of action, or legal remedy therefrom, of any person for injury or damage arising from any violation of this ordinance or from other law.

ARTICLE 11: SEVERABILITY

11.1. If any provision of this ordinance is held to be unconstitutional, preempted by federal law, or otherwise invalid by any court of competent jurisdiction, the remaining provisions of the ordinance shall not be invalidated.

ARTICLE 12: EFFECTIVE DATE

12.1. This ordinance shall take effect on _____.

Sources
Adapted from the following references:
Anon. 1977. *Model Noise Control Ordinance for Stationary Sources.* Trenton, NJ: New Jersey State Department of Environmental Protection and Energy.
Anon. 1977. *Model Community Noise Control Ordinance.* Berkeley, CA: California Department of Health Services Office of Noise Control.

INDEX

[References are to sections.]

A

AGENCY RULEMAKING
Federal administrative rulemaking
    History of . . . 3[A][1]
    Judicial review of . . . 3[A][6]
State administrative rulemaking (See STATE ADMIN-
  ISTRATIVE RULEMAKING, subhead: Agency
  rulemaking)

AMBIGUOUS WORDS
Generally . . . 11[B]
Elimination of ambiguity . . . 11[H]
Generality, elimination of over and under . . . 11[H]
Poor drafting, confusing ambiguity with . . . 11[G]
Unintended vagueness, elimination of . . . 11[H]

B

BILL SECTIONS, ARRANGEMENT OF
Examples of bills . . . App.
Implementing provisions
    Effective date . . . 7[C][4]
    Emergency . . . 7[C][5]
    Existing code, placement in . . . 7[C][1]
    Saving clause . . . 7[C][3]
    Severability . . . 7[C][2]
Letters and numbers, subdivision by . . . 7[E]
Mandatory provisions . . . 7[A]
Numbers, subdivision by letters and . . . 7[E]
Optional provisions
    Findings statement . . . 7[B][2]
    Policy . . . 7[B][2]
    Purpose . . . 7[B][2]
    Short title . . . 7[B][1]
Provisions
    Implementing (See subhead: Implementing pro-
    visions)
    Mandatory . . . 7[A]
    Optional (See subhead: Optional provisions)
Substantive sections . . . 7[D]

C

CAPITAL LETTERS
Generally . . . 13[C][6]

CHILDREN
Environmental health risks, and . . . 3[A][5][e]

COURTS
Rules
    Federal administrative rulemaking . . . 3[B]
    State rulemaking (See STATE COURT RULES)
Statutes and rules in court
    Canons of construction
        Limited to statutory/rule text . . . 5[E]

COURTS—Cont.
Statutes and rules in court—Cont.
    Canons of construction—Cont.
        Sources outside text, concerning . . . 5[F]
    Construction, meaning of . . . 5[A]
    Drafter, importance of statutory and rule inter-
      pretation to . . . 5[B]
    Interpretation
        Meaning of statutory . . . 5[A]
        Rules, of statutory . . . 5[C]
    Legislative history . . . 5[G]
    Literature on statutory rules . . . 5[D]

CROSS REFERENCE
Generally . . . 13[C][8]

D

DRAFTING PROCESS
Generally . . . Ch.9
Legal drafting (See LEGAL DRAFTING)
Provisions or words, rules on drafting (See PROVI-
  SIONS OR WORDS, RULES ON DRAFTING
  SPECIFIC)
Rule drafting
    Plain English in, critics of . . . 1[D]
    Problems of, special . . . 1[C]
Sentence drafting, Plain English principles and rules
  on (See SENTENCE DRAFTING, PLAIN ENG-
  LISH PRINCIPLES AND RULES ON)
Statutory drafting (See STATUTORY DRAFTING)

E

ENVIRONMENT
Children and environmental health risks
    . . . 3[A][5][e]
Executive orders
    Children and environmental health risks
        . . . 3[A][5][e]
    Environmental justice . . . 3[A][5][f]
    Health risks, children and . . . 3[A][5][e]
Health risks, children and . . . 3[A][5][e]
Impact on federal administrative rulemaking
    . . . 3[A][4][g]
Justice, environmental . . . 3[A][5][f]

F

FEDERAL ADMINISTRATIVE RULEMAKING
Advanced notice of proposed rulemaking
    . . . 3[A][3][a][ii]
Agency rulemaking
    History of . . . 3[A][1]
    Judicial review of . . . 3[A][6]
Authority, source of rulemaking . . . 3[A][2]
Benefit, cost versus . . . 3[A][5][a]

[References are to sections.]

MANDATORY FORM AND LANGUAGE—Cont.
Single subject . . . 6[C][3]
State
    Generally . . . 6[B]
    Identification and numbering system
      . . . 6[C][1][a]
Title . . . 6[C][3]

**MODEL STATE ADMINISTRATIVE PROCE-
DURE ACT** (See STATE ADMINISTRATIVE
RULEMAKING, subhead: Model State Administra-
tive Procedure Act)

O

ORDINANCE, BILLS AND
Examples of . . . 6[C][7]; App.

P

PETITION
State administrative rulemaking . . . 4[A][2][d][v]

PHRASES, MISUSED (See WORDS, subhead: Misused words and phrases)

PLAIN ENGLISH (GENERALLY)
Generally . . . 1[E]
Drafting process (See DRAFTING PROCESS)
Federal administrative rulemaking, statutory con-
    straints on . . . 3[A][4][c]
Sentence drafting, principles and rules on (See SEN-
    TENCE DRAFTING, PLAIN ENGLISH PRIN-
    CIPLES AND RULES ON)
Statutory constraints on federal administrative rule-
    making . . . 3[A][4][c]
Structure, style, and substance, relationship between
    . . . 8[B]
Substance, effect of structure and style on
    Structure, style, and substance, relationship be-
      tween . . . 8[B]
    Writing and thinking, relationship between
      . . . 8[A]
Thinking, relationship between writing and . . . 8[A]
Words (See WORDS)
Writing and thinking, relationship between . . . 8[A]

PREDICATE (See SENTENCE DRAFTING, PLAIN
ENGLISH PRINCIPLES AND RULES ON, subhead: Predicate)

PROPERTY RIGHTS
Generally . . . 3[A][5][g]

**PROVISIONS OR WORDS, RULES ON DRAFT-
ING SPECIFIC**
Generally . . . 13[A]
Age . . . 13[C][5][a]
Capital letters . . . 13[C][6]
Conditions
    Generally . . . 13[C][1]
    If . . . 13[C][1][a]
    When . . . 13[C][1][b]

**PROVISIONS OR WORDS, RULES ON DRAFT-
ING SPECIFIC**—Cont.
Conditions—Cont.
    Where . . . 13[C][1][c]
Cross reference . . . 13[C][8]
Date . . . 13[C][5][b]
Day . . . 13[C][5][b]
Definitions
    Exclude word defined from . . . 13[B][5]
    Include only words that are commonly under-
      stood to fit within word defined . . . 13[B][6]
    Means versus *includes* . . . 13[B][3]
    Placement of . . . 13[B][2]
    Substantive provisions with definition, not to
      include . . . 13[B][4]
    When to define . . . 13[B][1]
    Word defined from, exclusion of . . . 13[B][5]
Exceptions . . . 13[C][2]
Governmental entity or position, establishment of
    . . . 13[C][3]
Hyphen . . . 13[C][7]
Number . . . 13[C][5][c]
Penalty . . . 13[C][4]

PUNCTUATION
Subject and predicate, rules applicable to
    . . . 12[C][3][b]

R

RULE DRAFTING
Plain English in, critics of . . . 1[D]
Problems of, special . . . 1[C]

S

**SENTENCE DRAFTING, PLAIN ENGLISH
PRINCIPLES AND RULES ON**
Clarity, rules to aid
    Predicate (See subhead: Predicate)
    Subject, the (See subhead: Subject, the)
Predicate
    Rules on crafting subject and predicate (See sub-
      head: Rules on crafting subject and predicate,
      general)
    Shall, usage of . . . 12[C][2][b]
    Verb (See VERB, subhead: Predicate)
Principles, basic
    Short sentences, use . . . 12[A][2]
    Simple declarative sentence . . . 12[A][1]
Rules on crafting subject and predicate, general
    Generally . . . 12[B]
    Plural noun, subject as singular rather than
      . . . 12[B][1]
    Positive rather than negative form, sentence
      drafting in . . . 12[B][5]
    Punctuation . . . 12[C][3][b]
    Qualifier, placement of . . . 12[C][3][a]
    Subject as singular noun rather than plural noun
      . . . 12[B][1]
    Tabulation . . . 12[C][3][c]

[References are to sections.]

[References are to sections.]

W